MASTER THE™ DSST®

History of the Soviet Union Exam

About Peterson's

Peterson's® has been your trusted educational publisher for over 50 years. It's a milestone we're quite proud of, as we continue to offer the most accurate, dependable, high-quality educational content in the field, providing you with everything you need to succeed. No matter where you are on your academic or professional path, you can rely on Peterson's for its books, online information, expert test-prep tools, the most up-to-date education exploration data, and the highest quality career success resources—everything you need to achieve your education goals. For our complete line of products, visit www.petersons.com.

For more information, contact Peterson's, 8740 Lucent Blvd., Suite 400, Highlands Ranch, CO 80129; 800-338-3282 Ext. 54229; or find us online at **www.petersons.com**.

ISBN: 978-0-7689-4454-9

Printed in the United States of America

10 9 8 7 6 5 4 3 2 1   22   21   20

Contents

Before You Begin

HOW THIS BOOK IS ORGANIZED

Peterson's *Master the*™ *DSST*® *History of the Soviet Union Exam* provides a diagnostic test, subject-matter review, and a post-test.

- **Diagnostic Test**—Twenty multiple-choice questions, followed by an answer key with detailed answer explanations
- **Assessment Grid**—A chart designed to help you identify areas that you need to focus on based on your test results
- **Subject-Matter Review**—General overview of the exam subject, followed by a review of the relevant topics and terminology covered on the exam
- **Post-test**—Sixty multiple-choice questions, followed by an answer key and detailed answer explanations

The purpose of the diagnostic test is to help you figure out what you know—or don't know. The twenty multiple-choice questions are similar to the ones found on the DSST exam, and they should provide you with a good idea of what to expect. Once you take the diagnostic test, check your answers to see how you did. Included with each correct answer is a brief explanation regarding why a specific answer is correct, and in many cases, why other options are incorrect. Use the assessment grid to identify the questions you miss so that you can spend more time reviewing that information later. As with any exam, knowing your weak spots greatly improves your chances of success.

Following the diagnostic test is a subject-matter review. The review summarizes the various topics covered on the DSST exam. Key terms are defined; important concepts are explained; and when appropriate, examples are provided. As you read the review, some of the information may seem familiar while other information may seem foreign. Again, take note of the unfamiliar because that will most likely cause you problems on the actual exam.

After studying the subject-matter review, you should be ready for the post-test. The post-test contains sixty multiple-choice items, and it will serve as a dry run for the real DSST exam. There are complete answer explanations at the end of the test.

OTHER DSST® PRODUCTS BY PETERSON'S

Books, flashcards, practice tests, and videos available online at **www.petersons.com/testprep/dsst**

- Art of the Western World
- Astronomy
- Business Mathematics
- Business Ethics and Society
- Civil War and Reconstruction
- Computing and Information Technology
- Criminal Justice
- Environmental Science
- Ethics in America
- Ethics in Technology
- Foundations of Education
- Fundamentals of College Algebra
- Fundamentals of Counseling
- Fundamentals of Cybersecurity
- General Anthropology
- Health and Human Development
- History of the Soviet Union
- History of the Vietnam War
- Human Resource Management
- Introduction to Business
- Introduction to Geography
- Introduction to Geology
- Introduction to Law Enforcement
- Introduction to World Religions
- Lifespan Developmental Psychology
- Math for Liberal Arts
- Management Information Systems
- Money and Banking
- Organizational Behavior
- Personal Finance
- Principles of Advanced English Composition
- Principles of Finance
- Principles of Public Speaking
- Principles of Statistics
- Principles of Supervision
- Substance Abuse
- Technical Writing

Like what you see? Get unlimited access to Peterson's full catalog of DSST practice tests, instructional videos, flashcards and more for **75% off the first month!** Go to **www.petersons.com/testprep/dsst** and use coupon code **DSST2020** at checkout. Offer expires July 1, 2021.

Chapter 1

All About the DSST® Exam

WHAT IS DSST®?

Previously known as the DANTES Subject Standardized Tests, the DSST program provides the opportunity for individuals to earn college credit for what they have learned outside of the traditional classroom. Accepted or administered at more than 1,900 colleges and universities nationwide and approved by the American Council on Education (ACE), the DSST program enables individuals to use the knowledge they have acquired outside the classroom to accomplish their educational and professional goals.

WHY TAKE A DSST® EXAM?

DSST exams offer a way for you to save both time and money in your quest for a college education. Why enroll in a college course in a subject you already understand? For more than 30 years, the DSST program has offered the perfect solution for individuals who are knowledgeable in a specific subject and want to save both time and money. A passing score on a DSST exam provides physical evidence to universities of proficiency in a specific subject. More than 1,900 accredited and respected colleges and universities across the nation award undergraduate credit for passing scores on DSST exams. With the DSST program, individuals can shave months off the time it takes to earn a degree.

The DSST program offers numerous advantages for individuals in all stages of their educational development:

- Adult learners
- College students
- Military personnel

Adult learners desiring college degrees face unique circumstances—demanding work schedules, family responsibilities, and tight budgets. Yet adult learners also have years of valuable work experience that can frequently be applied toward a degree through the DSST program. For example, adult learners with on-the-job experience in business and management might be able to skip the Business 101 courses if they earn passing marks on DSST exams such as Introduction to Business and Principles of Supervision.

Adult learners can put their prior learning into action and move forward with more advanced course work. Adults who have never enrolled in a college course may feel a little uncertain about their abilities. If this describes your situation, then sign up for a DSST exam and see how you do. A passing score may be the boost you need to realize your dream of earning a degree. With family and work commitments, adult learners often feel they lack the time to attend college. The DSST program provides adult learners with the unique opportunity to work toward college degrees without the time constraints of semester-long course work. DSST exams take two hours or less to complete. In one weekend, you could earn credit for multiple college courses.

The DSST exams also benefit students who are already enrolled in a college or university. With college tuition costs on the rise, most students face financial challenges. The fee for each DSST exam starts at $80 (plus administration fees charged by some testing facilities)—significantly less than the $750 average cost of a 3-hour college class. Maximize tuition assistance by taking DSST exams for introductory or mandatory course work. Once you earn a passing score on a DSST exam, you are free to move on to higher-level course work in that subject matter, take desired electives, or focus on courses in a chosen major.

Not only do college students and adult learners profit from DSST exams, but military personnel reap the benefits as well. If you are a member of the armed services at home or abroad, you can initiate your post-military career by taking DSST exams in areas with which you have experience. Military personnel can gain credit anywhere in the world, thanks to the fact that almost all of the tests are available through the internet at designated testing locations. DSST testing facilities are located at more than 500 military installations, so service members on active duty can get a jump-start on a post-military career with the DSST program. As an additional incentive, DANTES (Defense Activity for Non-Traditional Education Support) provides funding for DSST test fees for eligible members of the military.

More than 30 subject-matter tests are available in the fields of Business, Humanities, Math, Physical Science, Social Sciences, and Technology.

Available DSST® Exams

Business	Social Sciences
Business Ethics and Society	A History of the Vietnam War
Business Mathematics	Art of the Western World
Computing and Information Technology	Criminal Justice
Human Resource Management	Foundations of Education
Introduction to Business	Fundamentals of Counseling
Management Information Systems	General Anthropology
Money and Banking	History of the Soviet Union
Organizational Behavior	Introduction to Geography
Personal Finance	Introduction to Law Enforcement
Principles of Finance	Lifespan Developmental Psychology
Principles of Supervision	Substance Abuse
	The Civil War and Reconstruction

Humanities	Physical Sciences
Ethics in America	Astronomy
Introduction to World Religions	Environment Science
Principles of Advanced English	Health and Human Development
Composition	Introduction to Geology
Principles of Public Speaking	

Math	Technology
Fundamentals of College Algebra	Ethics in Technology
Math for Liberal Arts	Fundamentals of Cybersecurity
Principles of Statistics	Technical Writing

As you can see from the table, the DSST program covers a wide variety of subjects. However, it is important to ask two questions before registering for a DSST exam.

1. Which universities or colleges award credit for passing DSST exams?
2. Which DSST exams are the most relevant to my desired degree and my experience?

Knowing which universities offer DSST credit is important. In all likelihood, a college in your area awards credit for DSST exams, but find out before taking an exam by contacting the university directly. Then review the list of DSST exams to determine which ones are most relevant to the degree you are seeking and to your base of knowledge. Schedule an appointment with your college adviser to determine which exams best fit your degree program and which college courses the DSST exams can replace. Advisers should also be able to tell you the minimum score required on the DSST exam to receive university credit.

DSST® TEST CENTERS

You can find DSST testing locations in community colleges and universities across the country. Check the DSST website (**www.getcollegecredit. com**) for a location near you or contact your local college or university to find out if the school administers DSST exams. Keep in mind that some universities and colleges administer DSST exams only to enrolled students. DSST testing is available to men and women in the armed services at more than 500 military installations around the world.

HOW TO REGISTER FOR A DSST® EXAM

Once you have located a nearby DSST testing facility, you need to contact the testing center to find out the exam administration schedule. Many centers are set up to administer tests via the internet, while others use printed materials. Almost all DSST exams are available as online tests, but the method used depends on the testing center. The cost for each DSST exam starts at $80, and many testing locations charge a fee to cover their costs for administering the tests. Credit cards are the only accepted payment method for taking online DSST exams. Credit card, certified check, and money order are acceptable payment methods for paper-and-pencil tests.

Test takers are allotted two score reports—one mailed to them and another mailed to a designated college or university, if requested. Online tests generate unofficial scores at the end of the test session, while individuals taking paper tests must wait four to six weeks for score reports.

PREPARING FOR A DSST® EXAM

Even though you are knowledgeable in a certain subject matter, you should still prepare for the test to ensure you achieve the highest score possible. The first step in studying for a DSST exam is to find out what will be on the specific test you have chosen. Information regarding test content is located on the DSST fact sheets, which can be downloaded at no cost from **www. getcollegecredit.com**. Each fact sheet outlines the topics covered on a subject-matter test, as well as the approximate percentage assigned to each topic. For example, questions on the History of the Soviet Union exam are distributed in the following way: Russia Under the Old Regime—10%, The Revolutionary Period 1914-1921—12%, Pre-War Stalinism—13%, The Second World War—14%, Postwar Stalinism—11%, The Khrushchev Years—10%, The Brezhnev Years—10%, and Reform and Collapse—20%.

In addition to the breakdown of topics on a DSST exam, the fact sheet also lists recommended reference materials. If you do not own the recommended books, then check college bookstores. Avoid paying high prices for new textbooks by looking online for used textbooks. Don't panic if you are unable to locate a specific textbook listed on the fact sheet; the textbooks are merely recommendations. Instead, search for comparable books used in university courses on the specific subject. Current editions are ideal, and it is a good idea to use at least two references when studying for a DSST exam. Of course, the subject matter provided in this book will be a sufficient review for most test takers. However, if you need additional information, then it is a good idea to have some of the reference materials at your disposal when preparing for a DSST exam.

Fact sheets include other useful information in addition to a list of reference materials and topics. Each fact sheet includes subject-specific sample questions like those you will encounter on the DSST exam. The sample questions provide an idea of the types of questions you can expect on the exam. Test questions are multiple-choice with one correct answer and three incorrect choices.

The fact sheet also includes information about the number of credit hours that ACE has recommended be awarded by colleges for a passing DSST exam score. However, you should keep in mind that not all universities and colleges adhere to the ACE recommendation for DSST credit hours. Some institutions require DSST exam scores higher than the minimum score recommended by ACE. Once you have acquired appropriate reference materials and you have the outline provided on the fact sheet, you are ready to start studying, which is where this book can help.

TEST DAY

After reviewing the material and taking practice tests, you are finally ready to take your DSST exam. Follow these tips for a successful test day experience.

1. **Arrive on time.** Not only is it courteous to arrive on time to the DSST testing facility, but it also allows plenty of time for you to take care of check-in procedures and settle into your surroundings.

2. **Bring identification.** DSST test facilities require that candidates bring a valid government-issued identification card with a current photo and signature. Acceptable forms of identification include a current driver's license, passport, military identification card, or state-issued identification card. Individuals who fail to bring proper identification to the DSST testing facility will not be allowed to take an exam.

3. **Bring the right supplies.** If your exam requires the use of a calculator, you may bring a calculator that meets the specifications. For paper-based exams, you may also bring No. 2 pencils with an eraser and black ballpoint pens. Regardless of the exam methodology, you are NOT allowed to bring reference or study materials, scratch paper, or electronics such as cell phones, personal handheld devices, cameras, alarm wrist watches, or tape recorders to the testing center.

4. **Take the test.** During the exam, take the time to read each question-and-answer option carefully. Eliminate the choices you know are incorrect to narrow the number of potential answers. If a question completely stumps you, take an educated guess and move on—remember that DSSTs are timed; you will have 2 hours to take the exam.

With the proper preparation, DSST exams will save you both time and money. So join the thousands of people who have already reaped the benefits of DSST exams and move closer than ever to your college degree.

HISTORY OF THE SOVIET UNION EXAM FACTS

The DSST® History of the Soviet Union exam consists of 100 multiple-choice questions that cover the history of the Soviet Union (the Union of Soviet Socialist Republics, or USSR) from its beginning in 1917, when the Bolshevik Party led by Vladimir Lenin overthrew Russia's Provisional Government, to its end in 1991, when the leaders of the three key constituent Soviet republics—Russia, Ukraine, and Belarus—signed an agreement to dissolve the USSR and induced its last president, Mikhail Gorbachev, to resign. The exam focuses upon the following topics: life under the Old Regime, the revolutionary period (1914–1921), prewar Stalinism, World War II, postwar Stalinism, the Khrushchev years, the Brezhnev era, and the Soviet Union's reform and collapse. Careful reading, critical thinking, and logical analysis will be as important as your knowledge of Soviet Union history.

Area or Course Equivalent: History of the Soviet Union
Level: Lower-level baccalaureate
Amount of Credit: 3 Semester Hours
Minimum Score: 400
Source: https://www.getcollegecredit.com/wp-content/assets/factsheets
/HistoryOfTheSovietUnion.pdf

I. Russia Under the Old Regime – 10%

    a. Governing institutions

    b. Economics

    c. Culture and society

    d. Foreign affairs

    e. Revolutionary movements

II. The Revolutionary Period 1914-1921 – 12%

    a. The first world war

    b. February/March revolution

    c. Interim

    d. Bolshevik revolution

    e. Civil war

    f. New Economic Policy (NEP)

III. Pre-War Stalinism – 13%

    a. Basic classical and Keynesian economics

    b. Monetarism and rational expectations

    c. Money and inflation

IV. The Second World War – 14%

    a. Pre-war foreign relations

    b. The course of the war

    c. The impact of the war

    d. Settlements of WWII and the origins of the Cold War

V. Postwar Stalinism – 11%

    a. Policy effectiveness

    b. Conducting monetary policy

    c. Interest rates and the impact on money supply

    d. Monetary vs. fiscal policy

    e. The financial crisis of 2008/2009

VI. The Khrushchev Years – 10%

    a. Succession struggle

    b. De-Stalinization

    c. Soviet relations with the U.S. under Khrushchev

    d. Rift with China

    e. Proxy Wars

VII. The Brezhnev Years – 10%

    a. Growth and stagnation

    b. Ideological dissent

    c. Detente

    d. Proxy wars in the Third World

    e. War in Afghanistan

VIII. Reform and Collapse – 20%

    a. Global challengers (Thatcher, Reagan, Pope John Paul II)

    b. External factors (Afghanistan, Islam)

    c. Perestroika and glasnost

    d. Reemergence of the nationalities issue

    e. Revolutions in eastern Europe

    f. End of the Union of Soviet Socialist Republics

    g. Gorbachev's legacy

Chapter 2

History of the Soviet Union Diagnostic Test

DIAGNOSTIC TEST ANSWER SHEET

1. Ⓐ Ⓑ Ⓒ Ⓓ   8. Ⓐ Ⓑ Ⓒ Ⓓ   15. Ⓐ Ⓑ Ⓒ Ⓓ

2. Ⓐ Ⓑ Ⓒ Ⓓ   9. Ⓐ Ⓑ Ⓒ Ⓓ   16. Ⓐ Ⓑ Ⓒ Ⓓ

3. Ⓐ Ⓑ Ⓒ Ⓓ   10. Ⓐ Ⓑ Ⓒ Ⓓ   17. Ⓐ Ⓑ Ⓒ Ⓓ

4. Ⓐ Ⓑ Ⓒ Ⓓ   11. Ⓐ Ⓑ Ⓒ Ⓓ   18. Ⓐ Ⓑ Ⓒ Ⓓ

5. Ⓐ Ⓑ Ⓒ Ⓓ   12. Ⓐ Ⓑ Ⓒ Ⓓ   19. Ⓐ Ⓑ Ⓒ Ⓓ

6. Ⓐ Ⓑ Ⓒ Ⓓ   13. Ⓐ Ⓑ Ⓒ Ⓓ   20. Ⓐ Ⓑ Ⓒ Ⓓ

7. Ⓐ Ⓑ Ⓒ Ⓓ   14. Ⓐ Ⓑ Ⓒ Ⓓ

HISTORY OF THE SOVIET UNION DIAGNOSTIC TEST

Directions: Carefully read each of the following 20 questions. Choose the best answer to each question and fill in the corresponding circle on the answer sheet. The Answer Key and Explanations can be found following this Diagnostic Test.

1. The imperial Russian army during the First World War

    A. was encircled and largely destroyed by the Germans in Eastern Ukraine.

    B. came close to capturing Berlin but stopped on the Oder River and was then routed.

    C. won all the major battles until crippled by Bolshevik agitation in 1917.

    D. retreated from Poland and Lithuania, but defeated Austria-Hungary in Galicia.

2. The Pale of Settlement imposed restrictions on which ethnic group?

    A. Finns

    B. Germans

    C. Jews

    D. Poles

3. One of the major decisions at the Yalta Conference in 1944 was that

    A. Poland would become a Communist republic.

    B. the USSR would stay out of the war against Japan.

    C. Communist war criminals would be amnestied.

    D. Germany would be subjected to demilitarization.

4. The Soviet collective farm system created in the late 1920s required villagers to

A. surrender most of their harvest to meet state procurement quotas.

B. grow only those crops that had military use, such as cotton or flax.

C. serve as a collective militia force to defend against enemy invasions.

D. engage in factory work for two months each year in addition to farming.

5. As the result of the 1941 Operation Barbarossa, the German military

A. completely cut off Allied supply routes into the Soviet Union.

B. caused the United States to enter the war on the Allied side.

C. inflicted huge losses on the Red Army but failed to defeat the Soviet Union.

D. captured Moscow and Leningrad and murdered most of their populations.

6. During the October Revolution of 1917, the Bolsheviks

A. forced Tsar Nicholas II to abdicate the throne.

B. overthrew the Provisional Government.

C. overthrew Kornilov's military dictatorship.

D. seized the leadership of the Petrograd Soviet.

7. The ultimate objective of the Five-Year Plans was to

A. create a modern industrial economy and make the USSR militarily competitive.

B. create an economy unhindered by post-WWI reparation payments.

C. create a large domestic market well supplied with food and consumer goods.

D. maximize the extraction of oil and coal to get cash for buying weapons.

8. The Revolution of 1905–1907 changed Russia's political system by

   A. depriving the tsar of all real power, now given to the Soviets.
   B. extending full political and civil rights to women and peasants.
   C. abolishing the State Duma and the Imperial Council of State.
   D. introducing a limited parliamentary system and basic civil rights.

9. Stalin's policy toward Yugoslavia in 1948 involved

   A. a conflict with Tito that effectively banished Yugoslavia from the Soviet bloc.
   B. tacitly supporting Tito's open invasion of Southern Greece.
   C. close alliance with Tito and a purge of anti-Stalin politicians in Yugoslavia.
   D. the removal of Tito by pro-Stalin politicians angered by his liberalism.

10. Gorbachev's policy of *glasnost* (openness) sought to

   A. open the Soviet Union's borders to tourism and commercial visitors.
   B. open up forced-labor camps in order to start relying on free labor.
   C. strengthen Communism through the public discussion of problems.
   D. expose Communist ideology for the failure that it really was.

11. The secret protocol to the Molotov-Ribbentrop Pact of 1939

   A. promised the Black Sea Straits to Stalin after victory over Britain.
   B. turned Czechoslovakia over to Hitler over British and French objections.
   C. negotiated the end of the Spanish Civil War of 1936–1939.
   D. divided much of Eastern Europe into Soviet and German spheres.

12. The Cuban missile crisis of 1962 broke out because

    A. Cubans stole missile technology from the Soviet Union to threaten the United States.
    B. the United States installed ballistic missiles in Guantanamo Bay to threaten Cuba.
    C. the United States Navy took over a ship with defecting Soviet and Cuban missile scientists.
    D. Soviet ballistic missiles, combat aircraft, and troops were deployed to Cuba.

13. The conflict between Armenia and Azerbaijan in 1988–1994 was over

    A. Nagorno-Karabakh.
    B. South Ossetia.
    C. the Donbass.
    D. Western Transnistria.

14. Stalin's nationality policies after 1945

    A. decided that Russian and Ukrainian languages should be merged.
    B. declared that victory had been achieved by all national groups working together.
    C. emphasized the leading role played by ethnic Russians in defeating Hitler's Germany.
    D. blamed Jews and Americans for causing Hitler's invasion.

15. What was the objective of the Soviet invasion of Afghanistan in 1979?

    A. To remove Hafizullah Amin from power and bolster the pro-Soviet regime
    B. To prevent an imminent Islamist coup by Nur Muhammad Taraki
    C. To install a Communist government that would be friendly to the USSR
    D. To gain access to a warm-water port on the Indian Ocean for the Soviet Navy

16. The objective of the attempted coup in August 1991 was to

    A. remove Communists from power.
    B. save the Soviet Union from collapse.
    C. turn the Soviet Union into a federation.
    D. expel Central Asian republics from the Soviet Union.

17. Khrushchev's "secret speech" of 1956 denounced

    A. Stalin's purges of loyal Bolsheviks.
    B. Stalin's forced collectivization of the late 1920s.
    C. deportations of ethnic Germans during the Second World War.
    D. his own incompetence during the Second World War.

18. The Cultural Revolution of the 1920s involved all of the following EXCEPT:

    A. Purging "bourgeois" academics, artists, and professionals
    B. Ensuring that Communist writers only used the Russian language
    C. Creative experimentation with form in all areas of the arts
    D. Creating the ideal of a "new" Communist individual

19. Brezhnev's leadership style as the General Secretary was to

    A. emulate Stalin's strong-man tactics.
    B. share power with his fellow Politburo members.
    C. delegate power to other ex-KGB men.
    D. give major positions to non-Party bureaucrats.

20. The Soviet leaders' initial reaction to Reagan's increase in military spending in the early 1980s was to become

    A. convinced that a major purge was required to uncover Reagan's spies.
    B. resigned to opening the Soviet Union up to capitalism and democracy.
    C. committed to providing Communist China with nuclear weapons.
    D. alarmed and determined to develop an adequate military response.

ANSWER KEY AND EXPLANATIONS

1. D	5. C	9. A	13. A	17. A
2. C	6. B	10. C	14. C	18. B
3. D	7. A	11. D	15. A	19. B
4. A	8. D	12. D	16. B	20. D

1. **The correct answer is D.** The Russian army retreated from Poland and Lithuania in 1915, but defeated Austria-Hungary in Galicia in 1914 and 1916. Choice A is incorrect because the Russian army was not fighting Germany in Eastern Ukraine. Choice B is incorrect because the Russian army did not come close to capturing Berlin. Choice C is incorrect because the Russian army did not win all the major battles.

2. **The correct answer is C.** The Pale of Settlement imposed civil and legal restrictions upon the Jews. Choices A, B, and D are incorrect because the Pale of Settlement did not apply to these groups.

3. **The correct answer is D.** Allies originally agreed that Germany would be deprived of its military forces and defense industry, though eventually both Eastern and Western Germany were rearmed. Choice A is incorrect because though Poland did soon become Communist, the agreement at Yalta was to hold free elections. Choice B is incorrect because the agreement was for the USSR to attack Japan after Hitler's defeat. Choice C is incorrect because Communist war criminals were not discussed at Yalta.

4. **The correct answer is A.** Collective farms were required to meet harsh grain procurement quotas. They could sell surplus product (if any). Choice B is incorrect because collective farms grew the entire range of agricultural crops cultivated in the Soviet Union. Choice C is incorrect because no military force was raised on collective farms. Choice D is incorrect because, although many villagers left to work in factories, this was not a required feature of collective farms.

5. **The correct answer is C.** The German army captured large amounts of territory and prisoners in the summer and fall of 1941 but failed to inflict a decisive defeat on the Red Army. Choice A is incorrect because Allied supply routes were not a major concern to Germany until 1942 and were never completely cut off. Choice B is incorrect because it was actually Germany that declared war on the United States and not directly as a result of Operation Barbarossa. Choice D is incorrect because Germany's military did kill large numbers of Soviet civilians but never captured Moscow or Leningrad.

6. **The correct answer is B.** In October 1917, Lenin's Bolsheviks overthrew the Provisional Government and seized power in the name of the Soviets. Choice A is incorrect because Nicholas II abdicated earlier, in February 1917. Choice C is incorrect because General Kornilov never became a military dictator. Choice D is incorrect because the Bolsheviks already controlled Petrograd's Soviet by October 1917.

7. **The correct answer is A.** Five-Year Plans were intended to catch up with the most advanced Western countries in industrial output and thus create the industrial capacity needed to upgrade the Soviet military. Choice B is incorrect because reparation payments were not imposed on the Soviet Union. Choice C is incorrect because developing a domestic market, including food and consumer goods, was not considered to be as important as infrastructure and heavy industry. Choice D is incorrect because oil exports were important in the 1930s but not the ultimate objective of Soviet industrialization; moreover, the USSR did not import large numbers of weapons.

8. The correct answer is D. The October Manifesto of 1905 granted basic civil rights, such as freedom of speech, religion, and assembly, and established a parliament consisting of the State Duma and the Council of State, which did not, however, have any control over the cabinet. Choice A is incorrect because the tsar retained control over the executive branch and Soviets were not officially recognized government organs. Choice B is incorrect because women and peasants did not receive full political and civil rights in 1905. Choice C is incorrect because the State Duma and the Council of State were not abolished.

9. The correct answer is A. Stalin's break with Tito turned Yugoslavia into a "nonaligned" nation equally distant from the West and the Soviet Union. Choice B is incorrect because Yugoslavia supported Communist guerillas in Greece but never openly invaded it. Choice C is incorrect because the Soviet Union's close alliance with Tito ended, rather than began, in 1948, and there was no Stalinist purge. Choice D is incorrect because while Tito's removal or even assassination was contemplated in Moscow, it was never carried out.

10. The correct answer is C. Gorbachev initially sought to revive Communism through more active public discussion and public participation in government. Choice A is incorrect because "openness" did not refer to open borders. Choice B is incorrect because Gorbachev's policies did not focus on the USSR's large (nonpolitical) prison inmate population. Choice D is incorrect because Gorbachev did not intend to undermine Communism itself.

11. The correct answer is D. The Pact recognized various parts of Eastern Europe as predominantly Soviet or German spheres of influence. Choice A is incorrect because the 1939 Pact did not promise the Black Sea Straits to Stalin. Choice B is incorrect because Czechoslovakia was turned over to Hitler as a consequence of the Munich Agreement of 1938, which was also signed by Britain and France. Choice C is incorrect because the Spanish Civil War ended in a Nationalist military victory and not a negotiated peace.

12. **The correct answer is D.** The 1962 crisis began after the United States found out that Soviet missiles and other forces were deployed to Cuba. Choice A is incorrect because Cuba did not steal missile technology from the Soviet Union. Choice B is incorrect because the United States did not install ballistic missiles in Guantanamo Bay. Choice C is incorrect.

13. **The correct answer is A.** The Armenian-Azeri war involved the region of Nagorno-Karabakh, which belonged to the Soviet republic of Azerbaijan but was largely populated by ethnic Armenians. Choices B, C, and D are incorrect because ethnic tensions in these regions did not involve the Armenians and the Azeri.

14. **The correct answer is C.** While recognizing other national groups and cultures, Stalinist propaganda immediately after the end of the Second World War claimed that the victory was primarily due to the efforts and sacrifices of the Russian nation. Choice A is incorrect because there was never any attempt to merge Russian and Ukrainian languages. Choice B is incorrect because Stalinist policies targeted several ethnic groups, such as the Chechens and the Crimean Tatars, for repression for their alleged collaboration with the Nazis. Choice D is incorrect because although Jews and Americans were indeed portrayed as opponents of the Soviet Union after 1945, they were not blamed for Hitler's invasion.

15. **The correct answer is A.** The Soviet invasion intended to bolster Soviet influence in Afghanistan by placing Soviet garrisons there and by removing Amin because he was thought to be plotting against the Soviet Union. Choice B is incorrect because Taraki was not pro-Iranian and was killed by Amin shortly before the Soviet invasion. Choice C is incorrect because Afghanistan already had a Communist government in 1979. Choice D is incorrect because Afghanistan did not have access to the Indian Ocean, and the Soviet government did not intend to invade Pakistan to obtain such access.

16. **The correct answer is B.** The members of Gorbachev's government who participated in the attempted coup intended to prevent the impending dissolution of the Soviet Union. Choice A is incorrect because the coup was not directed against Communists. Choice C is incorrect because it did not intend to turn the Soviet Union into a federation. Choice D is incorrect because the coup was attempted to save the Soviet Union, not to expel any of its constituent republics.

17. **The correct answer is A.** Khrushchev's "secret speech" condemned Stalin's purges of Bolsheviks who had been loyal to Stalin but did not apply to the purges of numerous other categories of victims. Choices B, C, and D are incorrect because Khrushchev did not address any of these issues in his speech.

18. **The correct answer is B.** New communist literature could be written in languages other than Russian, as long as it was socialist in content. Choices A, C, and D are incorrect because all of these items were part of the Cultural Revolution.

19. **The correct answer is B.** Brezhnev exercised his power through consensus with several other top Party members. Choice A is incorrect because although the cult of Stalin made a limited reappearance under Brezhnev, the latter did not imitate his ruling style. Choice C is incorrect because while the KGB and its chairman Yurii Andropov were important under Brezhnev, he himself was not a KGB man. Choice D is incorrect because membership in the Communist Party was required to hold any important position in the Soviet government.

20. **The correct answer is D.** Soviet leaders were alarmed by U.S. military spending and decided that more advanced military systems had to be designed to counter the latest U.S. weapons. Choice A is incorrect because some Soviet leaders believed that stricter discipline was needed but none of them wanted a major purge. Choice B is incorrect because Soviet leaders did not at any point think that changing the USSR's ideology or socioeconomic system was a proper response to U.S. military pressure. Choice C is incorrect because China already possessed nuclear weapons.

DIAGNOSTIC TEST ASSESSMENT GRID

Now that you've completed the diagnostic test and read through the answer explanations, you can use your results to target your studying. Find the question numbers from the diagnostic test that you answered incorrectly and highlight or circle them below. Then focus extra attention on the sections dealing with those topics.

History of the Soviet Union

Content Area	Topic	Question #
Russia Under the Old Regime	• Governing Institutions • Economics • Culture and Society • Foreign Affairs • Revolutionary Movements	2, 8
The Revolutionary Period: 1914–1921	• The First World War • February/March Revolution • Interim • Bolshevik Revolution • Civil War • New Economic Policy (NEP)	1, 6
Prewar Stalinism	• Collectivization • Industrialization • Reign of Terror • Stalinist Culture • Nationalities	4, 7, 18
The Second World War	• Prewar Foreign Relations • The Course of the War • The Impact of the War • Settlements of WWII and the Origins of the Cold War	3, 5, 11
Postwar Stalinism	• Reconstruction • Nationalism • The Arms Race • Cold War in Europe • Cold War in Asia	9, 14

The Khrushchev Years	• Succession Struggle • De-Stalinization • Soviet Relations with the U.S. Under Khrushchev • Proxy Wars • Rift with China	12, 17
The Brezhnev Era	• Growth and Stagnation • Ideological Dissent • Détente • Proxy Wars in the Third World • War in Afghanistan	15, 19
Reform and Collapse	• Global Challengers • External Factors (Afghanistan, Islam) • Perestroika and Glasnost • Reemergence of the Nationalities Issues • Revolutions in Eastern Europe • End of the Union of Soviet Socialist Republics • Gorbachev's Legacy	10, 13, 16, 20

Chapter 3

History of the Soviet Union Subject Review

RUSSIA UNDER THE OLD REGIME

Governing Institutions

The country known today as Russia first became powerful in the late fifteenth century, when the Grand Duchy of Moscow (also known as Muscovy) rose to prominence among dozens of small East Slavic states, known collectively as Rus'. Compared to its neighbors, such as Poland or the Mongol Empire, Muscovy was small, poor, and thinly populated. Yet, within a few generations, it became the largest state in Europe and eventually in the world. Traditionally referred to as "tsars," the rulers of Moscow claimed to be overlords of all the lands of medieval Rus', which today comprise European Russia, Ukraine, and Belarus (Belorussia). Tsar Peter the Great (r. 1682–1725) changed much of Russia's politics and culture in accordance with contemporary Western European models. He moved his capital from **Moscow** to the newly founded city of **St. Petersburg** on the Baltic Sea and in 1721 adopted the title of "emperor," intended to assert his equality with the grandest European rulers.

In the 1860s, Alexander II began his trailblazing reign as tsar as he completely overhauled the court system and the process of legal proceedings in an attempt to unify the judicial system, emancipated serfs, and allowed some localized self-government.

In the early twentieth century, Russia was the only major European state headed by a monarch who was not formally limited by an elected parliament or by any law that he could not change at will. The term for this type of rule is **autocracy**.) Russia's last tsar, **Nicholas II** (r. 1894-1917), was brought up believing that he had a divine mission to maintain his autocratic power.

> **TIP:** Many observers mistakenly thought Nicholas II to be weak-willed and easily swayed by advisers, but, in fact, despite his mild and soft-spoken manner, he was stubborn and determined to preserve his vast powers.

The Revolution of 1905–1907 and the Duma Monarchy

Only in 1905, facing massive labor strikes, urban riots, and military mutinies—the Revolution of 1905–1907—was Nicholas II persuaded to establish an elected legislature, the **State Duma**, with the power to control the budget and to grant his subjects' basic civil rights, including freedom of speech, worship, and assembly. Nonetheless, Nicholas retained important powers, which included control over all cabinet appointments, foreign policy, and provincial governors, thus limiting the parliamentary system. The **Russian Orthodox Church**, closely tied to the monarchy, remained Russia's state religion, although other faiths were tolerated even before 1905. Russia's judiciary was technically independent after the court reform of 1864 and, on the whole, managed to resist political pressure, except for cases involving revolutionary terrorism and propaganda, which were thought to be too sensitive to be tried by regular juries.

Economics

Russia's economy in the early twentieth century was one of the largest in the world, its GDP inferior only to the United States, Germany, and Great Britain and approximately equal to that of France. It was a leading exporter of agricultural products, for example, holding almost 40 percent of the export market for wheat. It was growing at a rate that was above average for Western countries and it was an attractive market for foreign investment. However, per capita incomes remained among the lowest in Europe.

Agriculture

The reason for the disparity between the size of Russia's economy and its small per-capita income was its mass of small-scale peasant farmers (over 85 percent of the population), whose labor productivity was much lower than that of Western European and American farmers. In central Russia, Ukraine, and Belorussia, peasants typically lived in **village communes**, whose leaders periodically redistributed plots of agricultural land among peasant families to ensure that they would be able to pay their share of taxes. In the **black-earth** regions of South Russia and Ukraine, agriculture was far more profitable than in the north, and huge capitalistic estates worked by hired laborers and owned by aristocrats or wealthy businessmen were common. In Central and Northern Russia, soils were poor, and peasants had to supplement their income by engaging in crafts and trade, finding factory work, or moving to cities.

In the late nineteenth century, peasants' productivity, prosperity, and health were gradually improving, and the population of the Russian empire skyrocketed from 129 million in 1897 to 175 million in 1914.

Nonetheless, the "**peasant question**" was one of the most pressing social problems in late imperial Russia, owing to the fact that rural areas were overpopulated and family land allotments were shrinking. The government attempted to solve this by promoting peasant migration and settlements of fertile lands in Siberia, the Far East, and today's Kazakhstan, but this strategy was only partially successful.

Industry and Trade

The first industrial enterprises appeared in Russia in the seventeenth century, and Peter the Great made an effort to establish a metalworking industry in the resource-rich **Ural Mountains**. In the nineteenth century, new economic centers had emerged:

- **St. Petersburg**, with its heavy and machine-building industry
- The **Moscow** area, with its textile and food-processing plants
- **Ukraine** and South **Russia**, with their rich natural resources and proximity to Black Sea ports

Not surprisingly, given Russia's size, its rail network was the largest in Europe in 1914. The **Trans-Siberian Railroad** connected European Russia to the Pacific Ocean, although it mostly had military, rather than economic, utility. Prior to 1914, the rail system was quite weak. Russia's financial system vastly improved with the introduction of the **gold standard** in 1897 by Finance Minister **Sergei Witte**. The gold standard held down inflation and encouraged investment by stabilizing the currency. In short, the economy in the early twentieth century had problems but overall was experiencing modern economic growth and was not at all a failure that could by itself explain the eventual Bolshevik Revolution of 1917.

Culture and Society

Imperial Russia had been for centuries divided into a system of **legal estates**, caste-like legal categories that included nobles, merchants, peasants, the clergy, and townspeople. These categories were usually inherited, but it was possible to change one's status and even become a noble through state service. The father of Vladimir Lenin, the founder of the Soviet state, became a nobleman by serving as a superintendent of a provincial school district.

Peasants were the largest such group or estate. Until the **Emancipation of 1861**, almost half of all peasants were *enserfed*, that is, tied to the land and treated little better than slaves: still considered to be moral human beings, serfs could nonetheless be punished at their master's discretion, sold, mortgaged, or even gambled away. After the Emancipation of 1861, almost all liberated serfs had to pay burdensome redemption payments to compensate their former owners for their loss. Noble landowners lost some of their land during the Emancipation but generally retained their wealth and their privileged access to education and state service. They also retained their power in the government in general, especially in the countryside among their former serfs. In addition, there was a growing middle class that included merchants, entrepreneurs, and various professionals.

Social Inequality

Many authors claim that the social gap between elites and common people in Russia was also a cultural one. Commoners were supposed to be truly Russian in their clothing, speech, and various social rituals, whereas the upper classes and the intellectuals—also known as the **intelligentsia**—supposedly had discarded their Russian heritage and embraced a common Western European culture. This picture is misleading, since even peasants actively participated in Russia's capitalist market economy, including its consumer culture, whereas nobles and rich merchants shared the Russian language and the Russian Orthodox faith and were also becoming more nationalistic on the eve of the First World War.

Foreign Affairs

Russia was among the victors at the **Congress of Vienna** (1814–1815), which concluded the Napoleonic Wars, but in turn lost the **Crimean War** (1853–1856) against Great Britain, France, the Ottoman Empire, and

Sardinia. Russia's defeat and subsequent military weakness facilitated the wars of German Unification. The rise of a powerful German state alarmed Russia and led to its unlikely alliance with republican France in 1893. Preparing to fight Germany in Europe, Russia was at the same time engaged in a competition with Great Britain in Central Asia known as the **Great Game**, with proxy wars and secret agents.

In the 1890s, Russia also intensified its efforts to develop and expand its Far Eastern possessions, coming into conflict with Japan in 1904–1905. It was a disaster for Russia, but it also enabled its army to learn from the defeat and to make a deal with Britain in 1908 that temporarily ended the Great Game. As a result, in 1914, Russia was a key member of the Triple Entente alongside Britain and France.

Revolutionary Movements

Ironically—given that the Bolsheviks would make Russia the world's first communist state—radical socialist parties in late tsarist Russia tended to be small and without any broad external support. Russia avoided involvement in the European revolutions of 1848. More widespread was the populist movement of the 1860s and 1870s. Building on the ideas of Alexander Herzen and Mikhail Bakunin, **populists** sought to achieve social transformation by working through the common people, especially peasants, who resisted attempts at radicalization. In desperation, some populists turned to terror to force the government to make concessions. Tsar **Alexander II** was hunted down and assassinated in 1881. While small in numbers, Russian radicals created an image of a professional rebel who would give up all normal occupations and attachments to focus on revolutionary work.

Revolutionary Parties and Marxism in Russia in the Early Twentieth Century

In the late 1880s, another influential radical group appeared, basing its views on the teachings of **Karl Marx**. Political change, according to Marxists, would be enacted by rebelling industrial workers, who were better educated and organized than peasants and were deprived of all property. Yet Russian factory workers were relatively few in number, and this raised questions about how to adapt Marx's teachings. Around 1914, populists were still very influential in Russia, forming the **Socialist Revolutionary Party**, or the **SRs**.

The Origins of the Bolshevik Party

The leading Marxist party was the Russian **Social Democratic Workers' Party**, who split in 1903 into **Bolsheviks** and **Mensheviks**. The Bolsheviks, led by **Vladimir Lenin**, falsely claimed to be the majority wing. Lenin's followers believed in forming a small core of dedicated professional revolutionaries and that other less dedicated socialist groups could be more dangerous than bourgeois oppressors. The Mensheviks—the "minority"—were led by **Yulii Martov** and were more inclined to use legal channels and to cooperate with other radical groups. These parties were very active during Russia's first revolution in 1905–1907, but after the tsar granted a constitution and basic civil rights, revolutionaries lost almost all of their mass support and tacit backing of the liberal propertied classes. Socialist leaders, like Joseph Stalin, were arrested or went into exile (Lenin or **Leon Trotsky**). Surviving groups were heavily infiltrated by tsarist spies.

THE REVOLUTIONARY PERIOD: 1914–1921

The long history of tsarist Russia came to its end during the First World War, 1914–1918, during which Russia fought on the side of the **Triple Entente**, allied with Great Britain and France, against the **Central Powers** of Germany, Austria-Hungary, the Ottoman Empire, and Bulgaria. Russia left the war early in 1918 as the result of a separate peace treaty. The war led to the collapse of Russian, German, Austro-Hungarian, and Ottoman multiethnic empires, and it also enabled the Bolsheviks to seize power in 1917 during the October Revolution. The Bolsheviks were able to consolidate their power and defeat their opponents during the civil war that began in 1918 and ended in 1920 (1922 in the Russian Far East).

The First World War

In 1914, Russia went to war with Germany and Austria-Hungary to protect Serbia, a small Orthodox Christian country in the Balkans, from an impending Austrian invasion. There were deeper reasons as well: an economic competition with Germany and geopolitical competition in the Balkans with Austria-Hungary. Russia's size made it very difficult to invade, while its huge population helped it to maintain the largest standing army in Europe. There are many myths about the imperial army's supposed inferiority and lack of weapons or training. In reality, it had many problems, but not more than every other European army.

The key weakness was the fact that the Russian economy as a whole, and especially its military industry, was too fragile to sustain a grueling war of attrition that tested industrial capacity and quickly devoured peacetime stocks of weapons and ammunitions.

Military Operations

During the opening battles, the Russian army had mixed success. One force attacked the German province of Eastern Prussia, while the Germans were busy invading France. However, the assault was hasty and poorly coordinated, and a smaller German force defeated General Samsonov's Second Army and captured about 50,000 prisoners. A clear and strategically important victory for Germany, the Battle of Tannenberg did not inflict any lasting damage on the Russian army.

At the same time, the Russians defeated Austro-Hungarian armies in Galicia, a borderland area in what is today Western Ukraine. But by the end of 1914, Russia's economy was barely coping with the war effort. Plans to increase production proved inadequate. Munition shortages became so acute in 1915 that the Russian artillery was unable to repel German offensives, which occupied Russian Poland and most of Lithuania. However, Germany failed in its objective to knock Russia out of the war or at least cripple it. In 1916, after the shortages were rectified, General **Aleksei Brusilov** inflicted a severe defeat on Austria-Hungary, and General Yudenich defeated the Ottoman Empire in Asia Minor. In sum, by the end of 1916, the military situation for Russia was stable despite severe losses. Some borderlands were lost to the Germans, but no major centers were captured or even threatened, as compared, for example, to France, which lost much of its industrial capacity to German attack.

Economy and Society During the War

Two other factors weakened Russia's war effort. First, its economic situation rapidly deteriorated. Tax revenues shrank, grain exports stopped due to enemy blockade, and inflation was rising, so that wages were losing their value. Conscription, refugee movements, and deportations of suspect groups (such as ethnic Germans) from areas close to the front created social dislocation. Second, politics and government were in a crisis. After the initial patriotic outburst, the losses of 1915 undermined the public's confidence in the tsar and his ministers. The Duma was convened only sporadically, and cabinet ministers were replaced every few months. There was no civilian leader on whom Nicholas II was willing to rely. In 1915, he even made himself a Commander-in-Chief—an unpopular move because it removed him from Petrograd (as St. Petersburg was renamed during the war).

Given the imperial family's withdrawn life and the absence of reliable information, rumors spread widely, blaming the Romanovs for military defeats and accusing the empress of being a German spy and a lover of the mystic **Grigorii Rasputin**. In short, Russia's elites no longer believed that the tsar could lead Russia to victory and avoid a serious crisis; they were willing to try something new.

February/March Revolution

The opportunity for change came in 1917. Economic problems and especially interruptions in food supplies in Petrograd led to strikes and then demonstrations and riots. The city garrison was ordered to fire on the protesters, but instead the soldiers started to join in. Nicholas II wanted to send loyal troops to regain control, but his top generals told him the revolution had gone too far and asked for his abdication. In March, Nicholas turned his throne over to his brother Michael who, in turn, immediately surrendered his power to a **Provisional Government** formed mostly by members of the liberal **Kadet (Constitutional Democratic) Party**. Nicholas and his wife and children were placed under house arrest and later transported to the interior of Russia to prevent them from fleeing the country. In 1918, they were executed by Bolshevik operatives in the city of Yekaterinburg.

Interim

The revolution in 1917 brought an end to centuries of tzarist autocracy. The sequence of events after Nicholas II's abdication served as milestones heading toward the communist revolution in Russia.

The Provisional Government's Policies and the Soviets

The Provisional Government's task was to govern until a **Constitutional Assembly** could be elected to determine Russia's new political structure. Meanwhile, it was to continue the war effort and make no major policy decisions. However, from the beginning this government had to operate in agreement with the **Petrograd Soviet**, a city council of deputies sent by factories and army units. Fearful that the Provisional Government would try to restore the "Old Regime," the Petrograd Soviet immediately issued its infamous **Order No. 1**, which created elected soldier committees in all military units (at first in Petrograd only but other garrisons soon followed their lead), whose authority superseded that of the officers. This decree crippled military discipline and thereby fatally undermined Russia's war effort. Soldiers started to surrender their trenches, refuse orders, murder their officers, or simply desert. Unlike the French Great Munity of 1917, Russian commanders were unable to restore order.

Lenin and the April Theses

The Soviet was dominated by socialists, mainly SRs and Mensheviks, as were the other Soviets that sprung up in most cities of the empire. The Bolsheviks initially played a minor role because most of their leaders were in exile abroad. Vladimir Lenin returned to Petrograd in April and issued his famous April Theses, in which he urged the Soviets to depose the Provisional Government; overturn the entire capitalist order, disband the army, the police, and the bureaucracy; nationalize all agricultural land; and refuse to support the war. This program met sharp criticism from the other parties and even from many Bolsheviks.

The July Days and the Kornilov Revolt

Many revolutionary leaders hoped that revolutionary ideas would improve morale and achieve a military breakthrough. However, the **June Offensive of 1917** was a great failure because, after initial successes, many units simply refused to advance. Only a few days later, this defeat led to another major uprising in Petrograd, known as the July Days. Started by conscripts trying to avoid being sent to the front, it was soon joined by the Bolsheviks. However, their first attempt to seize power through a mass popular uprising failed because their party lacked sufficient support and experience.

The result of the July Days was a rapid polarization of Russia's political life. The Bolsheviks were for a while viewed as traitors to the revolution. Liberal ministers were forced to resign and were replaced by moderate socialists led by former lawyer **Alexander Kerensky**. The military command was given to conservative General **Lavr Kornilov**, who was tasked with restoring military discipline. In late August, he sent some troops to Petrograd, apparently at Kerensky's request, to finish off the Bolsheviks and introduce direct military rule. However, Kerensky was reluctant to lose his power: he changed his mind and declared Kornilov a traitor. Kornilov's "rebellion" failed, but the Provisional Government lost most of its legitimacy, whereas the Soviets were becoming more influential and led by a resurgent Bolshevik party.

Bolshevik Revolution

Political crisis, lack of military success, and continuing economic decline all undermined the Provisional Government, and in October the Bolshevik Party organized a coup in the name of the Bolshevik-dominated Soviets. The Bolsheviks cooperated with the more radical members of the Social Revolutionary Party and enjoyed considerable support among the Petrograd garrison and among factory workers. Kerensky's government was unable to obtain emergency powers; most politicians also believed that the Bolsheviks' uprising would fail as it had in July.

Over the course of several days, Lenin's Bolsheviks seized control of the garrison, captured most militarily important points and finally, on November 7-8[1], arrested the Provisional Government itself without any significant bloodshed. This event became officially known as the Great October Socialist Revolution, or just the **October Revolution**. Two days later, Lenin formed a new government consisting only of Bolsheviks—the **Soviet of People's Commissars**. However, bloody street fighting continued in Moscow for another week and forces loyal to the Provisional Government continued to resist in many other cities. Elections to the Constitutional Assembly were held as planned. The result was that only about a quarter of all seats went to the Bolsheviks, and the Assembly was disbanded on its opening day, while a demonstration in its support was gunned down by Bolshevik troops. Meanwhile, the Soviets were purged of members who refused to support the Bolsheviks.

Bolshevik Policies and War Communism

Once they seized power, the Bolsheviks introduced a policy of "war communism" that was meant to jump-start Russia's crumbling government and the economy. Some measures were meant to win popular support, such as the declaration of the 8-hour workday, the placing of all factories under workers' control, and granting all ethnic groups the right of self-determination.

Other measures were meant to secure Bolshevik power: political parties and newspapers opposing the Bolsheviks were prohibited, and the old-regime army, state service, courts, and the police were all disbanded and replaced with a new Bolshevik-controlled military force. A December 20,

---

1 The dates November 7–8 correspond to the New Style (Gregorian) calendar. Until 1918, Soviet Russia used the Old Style (Julian) calendar, on which the dates of the revolution were October 24–25.

1917, decree established the ChK (or **Cheka**), the Bolshevik secret police tasked with fighting counterrevolution, suppressing economic crime, and combating corruption within the Soviet government.

Nationalization of Private Property

Most important, the policy of war communism also included claiming complete control over the economy, seizing all banks and their deposits, nationalizing all large industry, prohibiting private entrepreneurship, and asserting complete monopoly over food supply and food trade, sending out food requisition squads into the countryside to ensure that the army and the most important factories would stay supplied. Not surprisingly, such policies led to mass uprisings and to runaway inflation and a flourishing black market. Eventually, in 1921–1922, Russia experienced one of the most terrible famines in its history, with approximately 5 million deaths from starvation.

Separate Peace with Germany

Finally, on March 3, 1918, Bolshevik Russia signed a separate peace treaty, the **Treaty of Brest-Litovsk**, with Germany, whereby it lost vast territories, including Poland, Ukraine, Belorussia, Finland, and the Baltic provinces, with almost a third of its population and a large share of its economic capacity. Lenin's government promised to make huge reparation payments and to demobilize Russia's military forces. Because of its separate peace with Germany, Soviet Russia was not included among the victorious powers during the Versailles negotiations in 1919. Taken together, Lenin's early policies were costly and arguably a failure overall, but they permitted the Bolsheviks to consolidate their power and defeat their armed opponents during the Civil War that began in early 1918.

Civil War

Anti-Bolshevik organizations and armed resistance began to appear everywhere soon after the October Revolution, but the Bolsheviks were able to maintain control in central Russia and especially in Moscow and Petrograd, arresting many conspirators and instituting a regime of **Red Terror**, which involved seizing and executing hostages. Anti-Bolshevik forces, known as the Whites, were made up of monarchists, liberals, and socialist revolutionaries, and they were more successful in the borderland territories.

Most White armies were led by former tsarist commanders with military experience, foreign assistance, and control over some important resources. Other White movements attempted to unite Russia against the Bolsheviks; in the process, they vowed to preserve private property and to leave the question of Russia's constitution to an elected assembly to be convened after their victory.

This project was not popular among non-Russian groups, among whom the Whites had to operate, or even among the mostly anti-Bolshevik **Cossacks**. Many regions were controlled by rebels hostile both to the Bolsheviks' **Red Army** and to the Whites. These were ironically known as the Greens. By late 1920, the Red Army had won the Civil War in European Russia because the Bolsheviks controlled Russia's central core, were more successful in economic and military mobilization, and were able to attract or conscript many military and other experts from the Old Regime.

New Economic Policy (NEP)

Even after the Russian Civil War, "war communism" still dictated Soviet Russia's economic policy. As part of the policy, farmers and factory workers were ordered to produce food and goods, and these items were then taken and distributed at the discretion of the government. During the war, this distribution plan was in place to keep towns and troops stocked with food and weapons. The inefficient implementation of this policy was in part responsible for the devastating famine in 1921–1922. The resulting national discontent led to the development of a new economic policy for Russia.

Crisis of War Communism, 1920–1921

As the Civil War was nearing its end in 1920, other troubles plagued Soviet Russia. The newly independent Poland invaded Soviet Ukraine, Belorussia, and Lithuania, attempting to restore eighteenth-century borders. The Red Army counterattacked all the way to Warsaw, where it was, in turn, routed. The defeat in Poland cost Soviet Russia large swaths of territory and showed that Russia's army was exhausted after almost seven years of continuous warfare. Peasants were revolting throughout Russia, especially in the rich agricultural region around Tambov. Even revolutionary sailors in the Baltic fortress of Kronstadt revolted in early 1921, showing that the Bolsheviks were starting to lose support among their most faithful followers. Party members were beginning to quit, and many started to openly question Lenin's leadership.

Agriculture and Trade Under the New Economic Policy (NEP)

In March 1921, the Bolsheviks produced policies that reintroduced some aspects of capitalism in Russia that became known as the **New Economic Policy (NEP)**. Most important, food requisitioning was replaced by a fixed food tax, and the amount of grain confiscated from the peasants went down from 70 to 30 percent of the harvest. Peasant farmers were allowed to sell their surplus, as markets and private trade were once more permitted. NEP became something of a golden age for Russian peasants, because they were now free from the most restrictive policies of the Old Regime and the Bolsheviks. Much of housing stock and small businesses were privatized, as well. Some foreign companies were allowed to do business in Soviet Russia. After years of privation, consumer goods and entertainment became more accessible, especially for the new entrepreneurial and property-owning class known as **NEPmen**, who were mostly not Old-Regime capitalists, but ordinary peasants and workers enriched by NEP policies. Some Bolsheviks became despondent at the apparent restoration of capitalism, but others viewed it as only a temporarily setback.

Limitations of NEP

At the same time, this restoration of capitalism was limited in scale. Most important, Lenin was adamant not to relinquish the Bolshevik's political monopoly. Non-Party periodicals or non-Bolshevik political groups were strictly prohibited. SR leaders and religious figures were put on massive show trials in the early 1920s (although the former were not executed because of protests by European socialists). The political structure was regularized by the formation of the **Union of Soviet Socialist Republics** in 1922. This was formally a union of independent republics that had the right to secede but were controlled by the Red Army and through the Communist Party.

Moreover, the government retained control over large-scale industry, especially heavy industry, and foreign trade. By reserving these powers, the Bolsheviks would be able to reverse NEP when and if they chose to do so.

PREWAR STALINISM

After Lenin died in 1924, Joseph Stalin emerged as his most powerful successor, sidelining other Old Bolsheviks and forcing Leon Trotsky to emigrate. Stalin had been one of the key Bolshevik leaders in 1917, although his military record during the Civil War was not spotless. Stalin came to power because of his control of the Bolshevik Party bureaucracy and because of his ability to forge temporary tactical alliances with other key Party members.

Collectivization

In 1926–1927, peasants could not or would not produce enough grain to afford to purchase manufactured goods from the state (which were often overpriced and of poor quality). The state needed food for export and to supply growing cities, so this created the so-called **"scissors crisis."** A "Right" opposition led by Nikolai Bukharin wanted to raise procurement prices to incentivize the peasants, purchase grain abroad, and stop persecuting better-off peasants (known as **Kulaks**). Stalin rejected this solution. Instead, his policy was to create large, more profitable grain farms using modern machinery that would be controlled by the state. However, he instituted this plan with no clear law or instructions. Starting in 1927, young party members were sent from cities to force peasants to surrender their land, livestock, and farming equipment to cooperatives (known as **collective farms, kolkhoz,** or **state-owned "Soviet" farms, sovkhoz**).

Ultimately the state's objective was not only to transform small-scale peasant farms into highly productive cooperatives but also to transfer resources from agriculture to industry.

The Great Break and Peasants' Resistance

In 1929, Stalin announced the "**Great Break**," claiming that the Soviet Union now had sufficient resources for complete collectivization. This intensification resulted in increased peasant resistance, with violence in the countryside peaking from 1930–1933. Peasants killed their livestock rather than surrender it, refused to work, and even killed activists in open uprisings. The government responded with arrests, executions, and exile; approximately 2 million peasants were branded as "**kulaks**" and exiled to remote regions. In a 1930 speech using the phrase "**dizzy with success**," Stalin falsely put the blame for these excesses on Trotsky's followers occupying local administrative posts. The state abandoned its demand for immediate collectivization and many nonviable collective farms were disbanded, but later the same year, the process was forcefully renewed.

The Great Famine in 1932–1933

Bad weather in 1931–1932 compounded the problems caused by badly organized collective farms, decimated livestock, and insufficient seed stocks and resulted in large losses at harvest. State procurements were reduced somewhat (by 22 percent for grain), and grain exports—necessary for the state to obtain hard currency—were also reduced, but neither measure was enough to prevent famine in the winter of 1932–1933. Estimates of the number of victims vary from 2 to 8 million deaths, and overall approximately 40 million people were starving.

Holodomor in the Ukraine

As the center of large-scale specialized farming, responsible for 25 percent of grain production, Ukraine's large peasant population resisted collectivization fiercely and consequently suffered greatly in the famine, called the *Holodomor* in Ukrainian. Some believe that Russian Bolsheviks committed an intentional genocide of Ukrainians. However, the famine was equally brutal in Kazakhstan and Russia (Siberia, the Volga region, the North Caucasus, and former Cossack areas). The famine was certainly largely manmade, not simply through the wasteful policies of collectivization but also through the seizures of grain used to punish peasants for resistance. In addition to the famine, peasants were arrested in large numbers for supposed sabotage of the harvest, and those remaining in the famine areas were not allowed to flee to the cities. The following year, peasants were allowed small garden plots for their own use, and centralized oversight improved the management of kolkhozes. Harvests improved, but isolated famines continued to recur throughout the 1930s.

TIP: The literal translation of the Ukrainian word *Holodomor* is "death by forced starvation."

INDUSTRIALIZATION

One of the goals of collectivization was to provide food for the industrial workers inhabiting Soviet cities. After the Civil War, Russian heavy industry was less competitive than ever compared to the leading capitalist states, and the Bolsheviks feared invasion from capitalist powers at any time. At the same time, industrial workers were assumed to be the base of Bolshevik support. Stalin introduced the **First Five-Year Plan** for 1928–1932, which was meant to guide a process of rapid modernization of industry at the expense of the peasants (a plan similar to Trotsky's). In its original form, the plan was well thought out and realistic. It involved 1,500 sites, of which fifty consumed half of all state investment. The major types of projects constructed included:

- **Infrastructure:** canals, railroads, the Moscow metro
- **Energy:** especially hydroelectric power plants
- **Processing raw materials:** especially iron and steel production
- **Machine-building plants:** tractors, automobiles

A further aspect of the Plan was to develop technical education, and universal elementary education was introduced in 1930. Foreign experts were widely used to guide the process, especially from Germany and the United States. **Albert Kahn** alone got contracts for $2 billion, while whole factories were assembled in the United States and then moved to Russia. Industrial production grew rapidly, at a rate of 10–16 percent per year. By 1937, the Soviet Union was able to boast the second-largest industrial capacity in the world, second only to the United States.

Limitations of Central Planning

Once the plan was in place, the leadership continually revised its goals upward until it became entirely unrealistic, which led to faked statistics. The state also encouraged a movement to exceed the plan, which defeated the purpose of thinking out the process in advance. The **Stakhanov movement** consisted of workers using organizational techniques borrowed from Taylorism and Fordism to exceed quotas at the expense of other workers. The plans were also executed in part by forced labor. The Second Five-Year Plan, covering 1933–37, was somewhat more modest and had better results. Yet many of its projects were badly built or simply unnecessary. Agriculture suffered from the process, but the failures were blamed on so-called "traitors" and "saboteurs." These accusations helped to encourage a culture of purges and denunciations.

Industrialization and Consumer Goods

Another criticism of the Five-Year Plans was that they slanted toward heavy industry at the expense of developing the domestic market. Consumer goods were insufficient in this period, even for those with enough money. Instead, the state organized a distribution system for consumer goods and food rationing. A system like this had already existed during the Civil War, in which party members and other privileged categories received better packages, and similar inequalities persisted in the 1930s. In the long term, Stalin's industrialization has been seen as the greatest achievement of the Soviet period, but its legacy should be weighed in terms both of its costs and relative efficiency.

Reign of Terror

By the mid-1930s, many of the worst aspects of collectivization and industrialization were settling down, and life was becoming slightly better for many. Yet what followed, starting in 1933 and culminating in 1936–1938, were mass arrests, deportations, and executions of alleged domestic "enemies."

Origins of Terror

Mass state-organized terror as a political tool was not new: the Red Terror first appeared during the Civil War and targeted members of former elite groups, monarchists, clergy, capitalists, and members of rival parties, and during the Cultural Revolution certain "bourgeois specialists" were targeted (they were engineers and other professionals who joined the Bolsheviks but were suspect because their training had been under the tsars).

The Great Terror of 1936–1938 and the Moscow Show Trials

The Great Terror of 1936–38 was different because Bolsheviks themselves became victims, including prominent early members of the party. Much of the party's "Old Guard" had at some point in the 1920s been in opposition to Stalin and his policies and were targeted on these grounds. In 1937 especially, victims often included people completely loyal to Stalin and large numbers of the party apparatus.

Reasons for this purge no doubt included Stalin's personal paranoia, but it was also a means of consolidating control, especially over regions that in the early 1930s often resisted commands from Moscow.

Cases were crudely falsified, usually relying only on coerced testimony from the defendants themselves. Some trials were publicized "show trials," including three **Moscow Show Trials** that were widely watched abroad, resulting in the execution or imprisonment of a total of 54 defendants, ultimately including **Genrikh Yagoda**, the former head of the Soviet-Russian secret police, who had supervised the first of the show trials. Other trials took place in other cities, out of the spotlight. The majority of cases were secret extrajudicial prosecutions carried out by secret police tribunals without even perfunctory legal protections.

The Extent of the Great Terror

But these trials and prosecutions were only the tip of the iceberg. At the heart of the Great Terror were two massive operations. Their purpose seems to have been to liquidate potential "enemies within," who were seen as likely to turn against the Soviets in the event of a major war, and send millions to labor camps (collectively known as **GULAG**) to silence and punish the enemy while benefiting from their labor. In a departure from typical patterns, these purges were largely driven not by political rivalries or personal animosities but were planned from above and mostly carried out through lists approved by Stalin or regional authorities.

> **TIP:** GULAG was the acronym for the Russian words that translate to "main camp administration." At the height of its use, the GULAG system consisted of a combination of nearly 500 camps and labor colonies.

One action, **Order 00447**, created for each region minimum quotas of various undesirables, including former kulaks, White army personnel, former propertied classes, and even ordinary criminals, who were to be put into two categories: those who would be executed and those to be imprisoned. The other operation targeted numerous national minorities—including Germans, Poles, Finns, Serbs, Greeks, and Koreans—who were suspected of being capable of helping the enemy if the Soviet Union were attacked. In total, direct executions during the Great Terror probably numbered about 1 million. There were no legal protections and often no hearings or proceedings whatsoever, and bodies were buried in secret. Millions more were either sent to the aforementioned labor camps or simply lost their jobs or were forced to move to less prestigious and less prosperous regions. The secret police itself was heavily damaged by the purges, as was the Red Army, which lost virtually all of its top commanders and much of its mid-echelon, who were accused of being traitors and enemy spies.

Responsibility for the Great Terror

There is debate about the extent to which the Terror was initiated from the top. A key piece of evidence is that it was stopped immediately when Stalin gave the command. By 1939 many people who had helped to carry out Terror were themselves purged. Fabricated prosecutions and killings continued until after Stalin's death in 1953 but were much more limited for the rest of his rule. At the same time, denunciations from ordinary people played a role in how the secret police fulfilled (or exceeded) their quotas, and there was a large stratum of persons who benefited from the purges because they took the jobs of the victims. These younger people tended to be completely committed to the Soviet regime because they owed their education and rapid rise to it

Stalinist Culture

In addition to terror and the transformation of the economy and society, the Bolsheviks from the very beginning regarded culture and the arts as a key instrument of control and of socialist restructuring.

The Cultural Revolution

The term "cultural revolution" was used from 1917 onward. Many intellectuals welcomed the Revolution as an act of creative liberation. The 1920s was a period of cultural experimentation and creativity building on the achievements of pre-1917 **Russian Silver Age** culture. In this period, cinema flourished creatively, as did art, literature, music, and theater. Mass celebrations were organized to honor the Revolution, with the intention of luring people away from religious observance. Mass campaigns were waged against religion, consisting mainly of propaganda (periodicals, posters, and lectures) but also open persecution of the clergy and practicing believers, directed against all confessions. The arts were also employed to construct a cult of the Revolution and its heroes and promote the "new" communist individual. Additionally, there was an attempt to purge the bourgeois academics, artists, and professionals. Until around 1935, there was little emphasis on Stalin himself, but by the mid-1930s, a cult of his supposed revolutionary achievements (many of them imaginary) began to dominate.

Education and Mass Culture Under Socialism

Another key component of the cultural revolution was a campaign against illiteracy and for mass elementary education. In 1917, literacy rates in Russia had been among the lowest in Europe, but the Soviets organized a massive literacy drive, promoted continuing education, and instituted a system of affirmative action in favor of students from the working classes. This effort did result in huge gains in literacy and was widely popular. The new generation of children who went to school in this system also became acculturated to the new regime and its values.

Cultural revolution also applied to daily life and affected housing, leisure, and food. Old "bourgeois" forms, with their emphasis on privacy, gave way to public forms, built on the models of pre-1917 industrial settlements that were already overcrowded and therefore boasted little privacy. The new ideal was that socialization, eating, and entertainment should take place in public spaces, and their content should be carefully chosen to reflect socialist values.

Part of this effort was intended to liberate women from domestic chores associated with the bourgeois family model. Soviet women enjoyed full political and civil rights and were encouraged to get an education and enter the workforce, while the state intended to provide childcare and collective food preparation. In reality, the state often had difficulty following through on these provisions, leaving women with a "double burden" of work and family responsibilities.

Socialist Realism Under Stalin

When the term "socialist realism" began to be used to describe an artistic style approved by the regime around 1932, it signaled an end to the Revolution in art. The new emphasis was on traditional models in literature, painting, and other art forms. **Maxim Gorky**, a prominent pre-1917 writer, came back from exile and headed the **Union of Writers**, which provided privileges in getting published, money, and housing, but also enforced norms in style and content. These norms endorsed traditional literary forms, but the subject matter had to reflect the goal of building socialism. In daily life, as well, the mid-1930s signaled the "Great Retreat," in which socialist ideology was preserved but was merged with "traditional" (and largely popular) values, such as prohibiting abortion; a renewed emphasis on family, including the subordinate position of women; and attention paid to consumer goods, simple entertainment, sports, and health.

Nationalities

Imperial Russia had ruled over several hundred distinct ethnic groups, large and small. For the most part, its policies toward these groups were flexible and tended to involve limited recognition of local identity, including culture, language, religion, and accommodations with local elites. In the late nineteenth century, however, the government promoted a new policy of "**Russification**," which meant extending the use of the Russian language and conversion to Russian Orthodoxy in several strategically important areas, especially among groups still developing their modern national consciousness. This policy created resentment in some areas like Finland and Poland, while in other areas, it was combined with Russian settlement, as in Central Asia and in the Caucasus. Jews were confined to living within the "**Pale of Settlement**," an area in today's Poland, Ukraine, Lithuania, Belarus, and a few other areas. Jews converting to Christianity or falling under various exceptions were permitted to live outside the Pale but were generally discriminated against.

National Minorities Under Socialism

Most Marxists tended to neglect the importance of national and ethnic identity, but Stalin was exceptional in arguing that such identities were powerful and deeply rooted. In the 1920s, the Soviet government introduced many policies building on their early laws extending full tolerance and civil rights to all ethnic, national, and religious minorities. This was applied not only to large groups, such as Georgians, Ukrainians, or Volga Germans, but even to very small groups that then acquired semi-autonomous political units, including local government, schools, and other cultural institutions.

National literature, theater, and newspapers were promoted, sometimes causing tensions with the Russian majority. The one caveat was that national cultural leaders had to conform to socialist standards or risk being accused of "bourgeois nationalism" and on that basis possibly subjected to arrest or even execution. Prohibited activities included advocating for greater political autonomy or social arrangements different from those prescribed by the Soviet government. In the 1930s, after Stalin consolidated his power, the extent of national self-expression was circumscribed and the number of national units (autonomous regions and districts) was reduced, but the main principle of the Soviet Union being a multinational state was left untouched.

THE SECOND WORLD WAR

In 1917, many Bolsheviks, especially Leon Trotsky, believed that the Revolution in Russia would be followed by Communist revolutions elsewhere in Europe and eventually perhaps throughout the world. Groups and parties allied to the Bolsheviks were springing up everywhere, staging armed revolts in such places as Bavaria, Hungary, and Germany in the early 1920s. Their "internationalist" militancy made Bolsheviks feared by the property-owning classes throughout the world. Nonetheless, being a major military and economic power, the Soviet Union became intimately involved in international affairs in the 1920s and 1930s. In 1941, it was invaded by Nazi Germany and became one of the **Allied Powers** in the **Second World War**. Despite suffering heavy losses, the Red Army eventually defeated the German invasion and after 1945 was poised to become one of the world's two superpowers. The Soviet victory over Germany came to be viewed—in addition to the Revolution and the Civil War—as a key foundational event of Soviet history, and after the end of the Soviet Union, the **Victory Day**, celebrated in Russia on May 9, became its most important national holiday.

Prewar Foreign Relations

Soviet Russia emerged as an outcast in Europe's system of international relations, especially after it signed a separate peace treaty with Germany and refused to repay massive tsarist foreign loans. After the First World War, several independent nations emerged from the ruins of the Russian, German, Austro-Hungarian, and Ottoman empires, all of them hostile to the Bolsheviks. In Western Europe, they were viewed as a buffer against a Communist threat.

At the same time, Lenin's government successfully found a way out of this isolation: first, in 1921, Soviet Russia signed the **Moscow Treaty** with the emerging nationalist Turkish government of Mustafa Kemal, providing him with money and weapons. In that year, Soviet Russia also signed a trade treaty with Great Britain, which thereby recognized the new government in fact, though not officially. Finally, in April of 1922, Soviet Russia signed a key **Treaty of Rapallo** with the German Weimar Republic, Germany thus becoming the first major nation to formally recognize the Bolsheviks. Russia and Germany gave up all financial claims against each other and agreed to cooperate in several military projects. On December 30, 1922, Soviet Russia, the Transcaucasian Socialist Federative Soviet Republic (Armenia, Azerbaijan, and Georgia), the Soviet Socialist Republic of Ukraine, and the Soviet Socialist Republic of Byelorussia signed a treaty creating the **Union of Soviet Socialist Republics (USSR)**, commonly known as the **Soviet Union**. During the 1920s, the Soviet Union was recognized by most major countries, although the United States did so only in 1933.

Foreign Relations in the 1930s

Soviet industrialization in the late 1920s and early 1930s largely relied on technical expertise and, indirectly (through grain exports), money from the West. Many Western European countries and the U.S. also had active socialist and communist movements that sought to turn their nations' public opinion in the Soviet Union's favor. After Hitler came to power in 1933, the Soviet Union began to participate in Europe's security arrangements, for example, through a loose mutual aid treaty with France in 1935. Nonetheless, Stalin and his government felt that Britain and France were unreliable as potential partners in a war against Hitler because of their pattern of failing to oppose Hitler's and Mussolini's advances in Ethiopia in 1935–36, in Spain during the Spanish Civil War in 1936–39, and during the Munich Crisis of 1938, when the USSR was excluded from the negotiations that handed Czechoslovakia over to Hitler.

The Molotov-Ribbentrop Pact

Although Stalin was wary of Hitler's avowed ambition to invade and colonize the Soviet Union, he ultimately chose to come to an agreement with him on August 23, 1939, signed as a **Soviet-German Nonaggression Treaty**, also known as the **Molotov-Ribbentrop Pact**, named for the two countries' respective foreign ministers. It contained a secret addition (or protocol) that divided much of Eastern Europe (Poland, Lithuania, Latvia, Estonia, Finland, and Romania) into Soviet and German spheres of influence. The Pact was not a formal alliance, and it did not require the USSR or Germany to invade any other country, even if the other side was attacked. It was, however, accompanied by economic treaties that supplied Germany with strategic raw materials in exchange for technological transfers. Britain and France began to regard Stalin as Hitler's ally and, after the beginning of the Second World War, started to make plans to attack objectives in the Soviet Union, such as the oil fields in Baku, to prevent them from benefiting Hitler.

The Pact in Action: Poland, the Baltic Republics, and the Winter War

After Hitler invaded Poland on September 1, 1939, Stalin waited until September 17, when Polish defeat was imminent, to order his troops to occupy Poland east of the so-called Curzon line, separating territories with primarily Ukrainian and Belorussian populations from the core Polish lands. While welcomed by some from the perspective of ethnic self-determination, the Soviet move resulted in rapid "sovietization" of these territories, with private property being nationalized and individuals suspected of anti-Soviet sentiments being arrested and deported or even executed.

Large numbers of Polish soldiers surrendered to the Red Army, and in 1940 over 20,000 Polish citizens, mostly captured military officers, were executed by the secret police without a trial in an action known as the **Katyn' Massacre**.

In the fall of 1939, Stalin coerced the authoritarian governments of the three Baltic republics (Estonia, Latvia, and Lithuania) to accept Soviet garrisons and, in 1940, forced them to appoint pro-Soviet cabinets and hold falsified elections, after which all three nations formally became constituent republics in the Soviet Union. Stalin's plans were less successful in Finland, another former part of the tsarist empire: After the USSR provoked a war in November of 1939, the small and poorly armed Finnish army effectively resisted the Red Army's attacks in the so-called **Winter War**. Although the Red Army defeated Finland in the spring of 1940, the war created the impression in the West that the Soviet Union was weak militarily as it did not gain the region of Karelia, and the successful, prolonged Finnish resistance provided a perception that ignored the Red Army's adaptability and high morale.

The Course of the War

As World War II progressed, the USSR and Germany found occasions to modify the conditions of the pact, adjusting borders of occupied territories and addressing trade, shipping rights, and immigration issues. The union was often uneasy, and it began to deteriorate with the USSR's invasion of Bukovina, Romania, in 1940, which was located beyond the USSR's agreed-upon sphere of influence. But Nazi Germany's actions on June 22, 1941, would terminate the pact once and for all.

The Origins of Operation Barbarossa

Hitler began making plans to invade the USSR immediately after the fall of France in July 1940. He had never made a secret of his view of Russians as racially inferior beings destined to be colonized and exploited by Germans. Subsequently, he (as well as some Cold-War propagandists after the fact) claimed that the Nazi invasion, **Operation Barbarossa**, was preventive because of Stalin's own massive war preparations.

However, there is no evidence that Stalin actively planned such an attack. Hitler viewed the Red Army as weaker than the French one he had already beaten and intended to defeat it in a few weeks using rapid advances of his mechanized forces, supported by aircraft. German intelligence about Soviet military capabilities was poor and colored by ideological prejudice. At the same time, Stalin and his government knew that Hitler was about to attack but did not know the details and received reliable information only when it was too late to mobilize.

After the war, the Soviets created a myth that the Nazi attack was a complete surprise because Stalin trusted in his treaty with Hitler. Another myth is that the Red Army was poorly armed. In fact, in 1941, it had more armor and aircraft than the rest of the world combined. Though many of these were outdated, they were not obsolete, and up-to-date models were about as numerous as the German front-line strength. At the same time, though, the army's organization, doctrine, and training had suffered from the effect of the purges in the late 1930s and from rapid expansion and frequent reorganizations.

When Hitler's army began its attack on Sunday, June 22, 1941, the Soviet leadership expected that the Red Army would immediately counterattack and repel the invasion. Instead, German troops penetrated deeply behind Soviet lines and within a few days captured Belorussia and were beginning to threaten approaches to Leningrad. Hundreds of thousands of soldiers found themselves encircled and most became POWs. Despite its huge losses, the Red Army continued to fight and disrupted German plans.

The German assault against Moscow began on September 30, and it failed to capture the city. Soviet reserves began a counteroffensive in December and drove the Germans back in what was the first major Allied victory against Germany. Operation Barbarossa had failed.

From Moscow to Stalingrad, 1941–1942

In spite of its defeat of Operation Barbarossa, at the same time, the USSR failed to turn this victory into a rout, and, in the spring of 1942, Hitler was ready to attack once again, this time only in the southern portion of the front. His target was the city of Stalingrad (present-day Volgograd) on the Volga, important not only for its symbolic value but also because of its strategic location. Another army force turned south, trying to capture the oil fields in the Caucasus. Due to the strength of Soviet resistance, Germans were unable to reach either of these objectives, and in November, their Sixth Army was surrounded in Stalingrad and soon capitulated together with its commander.

The Soviet Victory

Stalingrad was a major victory for the Red Army, but elsewhere it was less successful: in the north, it failed to lift the German siege of Leningrad, a major war crime that caused over 600,000 civilian deaths from starvation. And northwest of Moscow, the Red Army failed to capture the Rzhev salient threatening the capital, despite repeated bloody assaults that resulted in over a million dead and wounded soldiers. In 1943, the German army once again regrouped and launched another assault near the South Russian town of Kursk in July. Known as one of the largest armored battles in history, Kursk was a decisive loss for the Nazis. Between July 1943 and May 1945, the Red Army went on an offensive that the Germans were unable to repel—despite their desperate attempts to launch a "total war." In particular, the Soviet offensive in Belorussia, Operation Bagration, begun on June 22, 1944, rapidly overwhelmed the Germans and advanced into German-occupied Poland. In April 1945, the Red Army surrounded and stormed Berlin, whereas to the north and to the south of the city its soldiers met British and American troops on the river Elbe.

USSR's War Against Japan, 1945

Although the war in Europe was over in August 1945, the Soviet Union declared war on Japan to fulfill its pledge to its Western Allies. Within days, the Red Army destroyed Japan's powerful Kwantung Army and occupied Manchuria, North Korea, Sakhalin, and the Kuril Islands.

The Impact of the War

During the war, the Soviet government continued to rely on existing mechanisms of coercion and ideological indoctrination, emphasizing the leading role of Stalin and the Communist Party and arguing that the war was started by German capitalists. However, these mechanisms were insufficient, and the state furthered the ideological and symbolic changes already begun in the 1930s. Stalin appealed to traditional Russian patriotism and used imperial-era heroes, such as Generals Suvorov and Kutuzov, as models.

Imperial-era military symbols were revived: uniforms were made according to pre-1917 patterns and officers' golden shoulder-badges were reintroduced in 1943. Religion, especially in the form of the Russian Orthodox Church, was rehabilitated, and surviving bishops met with Stalin and were allowed to elect a Patriarch. Although some military commanders blamed for the June 1941 defeat were executed, many purge victims from 1939–1940 were freed and allowed to join the army.

Industrial Mobilization; Women and Children

Even before the German invasion, large segments of the Soviet economy operated on a wartime footing, and the major impact of the attack was to continue the process of mobilization. This affected above all those civilian productive capacities that could be altered to produce military equipment and supplies. Immediately after the war began, Stalin ordered the evacuation of key military industries from the western regions of the USSR to the Urals and Siberia. But the German advance was so rapid that only around 10 percent of industry could be removed from affected areas. Evacuees often found themselves in open fields without any of their possessions. Those factories that remained operational had to rely on the labor of women and children. Most civilians, and especially those engaged in agriculture, were given low priority in receiving supplies and suffered extensive privations, even when they were not exposed to direct military action.

Soviet Losses

The USSR overall lost about 30 percent of its national wealth, and territories occupied by Germany lost about two-thirds. Approximately 4 million civilians died from hunger, disease, lack of medical care, and other privations. German soldiers were permitted to kill and molest Soviet civilians with impunity, and so losses were much greater for those directly affected by the invasion: almost 7.5 million civilians were murdered on occupied territory or died from enemy actions such as artillery strikes and bombing. Over 2 million more died performing slave labor in Germany, and more than 1.5 million Soviet POWs died.

In addition, a mass famine occurred in 1946, resulting in 1 to 1.5 million deaths. Two million people were war invalids who would not see much public assistance from their post-war government. In addition, the **Holocaust** was carried out partially on Soviet territory. Approximately 3 million Jews were in German-occupied parts of the USSR, and their mass murder began shortly after the invasion, with the assistance of local collaborators. There were several sites of mass execution, most notably **Babi Yar** in Kiev, where over 100,000 Jews were executed.

Settlements of WWII and the Origins of the Cold War

The Soviet Union joined the **Atlantic Charter** in 1941. During the war, Stalin held three conferences with the leaders of Britain and the United States that decided on the post-war settlement (Tehran Conference in 1943; Yalta Conference and Potsdam Conference in 1945). The territorial rearrangement that emerged from these negotiations moved Poland's border westward, gave the USSR one-third of Eastern Prussia, demilitarized the German army, reduced German territory by 25 percent, and divided it into occupation zones. The USSR was also granted Japanese territories lost by Russia in 1905.

In addition, the Soviet Union joined in an agreement to create the United Nations, which gave the USSR the legitimacy of occupying a key position in the most important international organization throughout the Cold War.

The Origins of the Cold War

Post-war settlements also laid the foundation for the Cold War by creating a bipolar division of Europe and eventually the world into two spheres of interest, or blocs. The USSR was in effect allowed to control Eastern (and most of southeastern Europe,) but disagreements emerged quickly about Poland, the status of the Turkish Straits, Truman's nuclear threat, and more. The U.S. and Britain both desired influence in Eastern Europe but eventually settled for keeping the USSR out of having any say in Western Europe, such as West Germany, France, Italy, and Belgium.

POSTWAR STALINISM

While facing the task of rebuilding its war-shattered country after 1945, Stalin's regime partially returned to policies of repression, which continued until Stalin's death in 1953. The predominant post-war ideology of "Soviet patriotism" blended the existing Communist images and stories with the more traditional mythology of Russian nationalism.

Reconstruction

Stalin rejected U.S. assistance from the **Marshall Plan**, believing its terms to be overly constraining economically and politically. Resources for rebuilding the Soviet economy included reparations from the Axis countries and forced labor (including that of POWs), but it was done primarily through continuing or even increasing the regime of total mobilization. The extensive black market that had been tolerated during the war was restricted again, but work continued to be carried out disproportionately by women and teenagers. In the post-war period, many families were headed by single mothers, since there were about 13 million fewer men than women in the age bracket between 20 and 44.

Less easy to measure is the psychological effect of years of extreme deprivation and trauma affecting the entire population. There were also long-term health effects: a contemporary study of working teenagers found that 35 percent were chronically ill. Much of Soviet housing stock was destroyed, and millions of people were dislocated through evacuation, forced displacement, or mobilization. The post-war period also saw a rise in violent and organized crime, especially in the larger cities.

....

TIP: Czechoslovakia, the Soviet Union, Bulgaria, Romania, East Germany, Poland, and Albania comprised the Communist Bloc during the Cold War.

....

Nationalism

Stalin's "Great Retreat" reached its high point after 1945, further developing the "Soviet patriotism" by mixing traditional Russo-centric civic nationalism and Communist ideology stripped of its internationalist aspects. Soviet patriotism used many traditional Russian symbols of power, historical figures, and monumental art, but was different in that writers and artists (such as Alexander Tvardovskii) who appeared too nationalist were chastised. Yet, intellectuals thought not to share these values—especially the poet Anna Akhmatova and satirist Mikhail Zoshchenko—faced brutal criticism by the Party and ostracism by their colleagues.

One particular element of this campaign was directed against Western (especially American) cultural and intellectual influences and targeted Jewish intellectuals, referring to them negatively as "Cosmopolitans." Almost all Jewish political and cultural organizations such as theaters were shut down. Shortly before Stalin's death, his secret police concocted the **Doctors' Plot of 1953** and arrested several physicians, most of them Jewish, for allegedly plotting to kill leading government figures. They were freed shortly after Stalin died.

The Arms Race and the Cold War in Europe and Asia

While British and American forces remained in Western Europe, the Red Army (partially demobilized but still large) occupied Eastern Europe. After the war, the Soviet Union committed to huge expenditures on new types of weapons: jet aircraft, missiles, radars, and especially nuclear weapons. The first Soviet nuclear weapon was successfully produced in 1949.

The Beginning of the Cold War in Europe

It was unclear in the first few years after the war what relations would be like between the USSR and the West. But President Truman was staunchly anti-Soviet, and Stalin took Churchill's 1946 "Iron Curtain" speech as a dangerous sign of the West's intentions. "Iron Curtain" referred to the fact that Stalin's government severely restricted travel from its sphere of influence and shut down almost all non-Communist political activities in the countries under its occupation. In a series of foreign policy crises, Stalin was careful not to overextend himself in the Greek Civil War, 1946–49, and the Iran crisis in 1946; however he did try to "Sovietize" both nations. On the other hand, he did stumble through some miscalculations: when Yugoslavia under Josip Tito broke from Soviet influence in 1948 and Stalin banished Yugoslavia from the Soviet bloc, and also the Berlin blockade (1948–49) that secured West Berlin for the Western powers and hastened the formation of NATO, an anti-Soviet military alliance. Stalin had ordered the blockade of Western-provided supplies to the people of West Berlin. Committed to reaching western Germans, the Americans and British circumvented the blockade and airlifted supplies, highlighting Stalin's miscalculation of the Western bloc's resolve. West Germany was then established in 1949, prompting the USSR to set up East Germany later the same year.

Soviet Rule in Eastern Europe

Stalin was more successful in Eastern Europe, where anti-Soviet guerillas were defeated all over, including in western parts of the Soviet Union itself. Pro-Soviet regimes were consolidated in Poland, Czechoslovakia, Hungary, Romania, and Bulgaria. Czechoslovakia was the most pro-Soviet of the satellite nations. These quickly became mini-Stalinist regimes with purges and secret police, where non-Communists, and then non-Stalinist communists, were often tried and executed.

Cold War in Asia, 1945–1953

Another key event was the victory of Chinese Communists in 1949. Mao Zedong was friendly to the USSR and dependent on its assistance. More questionable in its effects for the Soviet Union was the Korean War, 1950–53 (ending in July, a few months after Stalin's death). The USSR did not officially take part, but it did finance North Korea and supplied Chinese troops. Approximately 30,000 Soviet soldiers took some part, especially manning aircraft during a massive air war between U.S. and Soviet planes. For the USSR, the war was mostly a failure because it did not unite Korea. But it increased Soviet authority in third-world countries, where the USSR came to be seen as a potential source of real military and economic assistance.

THE KHRUSHCHEV YEARS

Nikita Khrushchev's rule (1953–1964) is usually interpreted as a period of relative liberalism, marked by the cultural "Thaw" and de-Stalinization. However, Khrushchev left intact, and indeed reaffirmed, the foundations of the Soviet regime, though he avoided the mass terror of Stalin's rule. In this style, he was able to gain and preserve his power by appealing to the Central Committee of the Party, as well as the army and the KGB. Khrushchev's unpredictability and mistakes in domestic and foreign policy eventually led to his removal by his close associates in the Communist Party.

Succession Struggle and De-Stalinization

After Stalin's death on March 5, 1953, a struggle for leadership took place among **Lavrentiy Beria** (the head of the secret police), **Georgi Malenkov** (the head of the government), and **Nikita Khrushchev** (the Moscow party boss). Malenkov and Beria traditionally worked together, but Khrushchev managed to divide them and organize what was essentially a coup against Beria. Beria was arrested on June 26 and was most likely murdered on that same day. In September, Khrushchev was elected as the First Secretary of the Communist Party.

Stalin's Cult of Personality Dismantled

At the height of his rule, Joseph Stalin was portrayed by the Soviet press as the all-powerful and all-knowing Father of the Nations. He was revered by the people in communist countries. Expressions of devotion permeated

all forms of media and his likeness was displayed everywhere. In Khrushchev's speech, "On the Cult of Personality and Its Consequences,"(commonly known as the **Secret Speech**), given at the 20th Party Congress on
February 25, 1956, he condemned Stalin charging him with having encouraged a leadership personality cult despite his claims of maintaining support for the ideals of Marxist-Leninist communism. Khrushchev referred
to this overwhelming cultural influence as Stalin's cult of the individual
The "Secret Speech" initiated a political reform, known as De-Stalinization, that sought to eradicate Stalin's influence on the Soviet society.

In addition, Khrushchev criticized Stalin's reign of terror but mentioned
only Stalin's persecution of Party personnel. Khrushchev said nothing
about collectivization or the Soviet ex-POWs who had been put in filtration
camps; former "opposition" members who had been purged, like Bukharin,
were also not defended. Still, the overwhelming picture provided by the
speech was of mass illegality, falsified evidence, torture, and extrajudicial
killings, with an emphasis on Stalin's personal responsibility.

Khrushchev Criticized

Although officially secret, the speech was nonetheless widely circulated.
Congress delegates were shocked, and many were dismayed. In June 1957,
an "**Anti-Party group**" comprised of older, leading Stalin-era Communists (Molotov, Malenkov, Kaganovich, Voroshilov) attempted to remove
Khrushchev from power. The KGB and the army, led by war hero **Marshal
Zhukov**, helped Khrushchev to resist the coup attempt. But in the after-
math, the USSR started having more problems with its satellites. Stalinist
Communists in Eastern Europe were also displeased with the new direction. In 1956 there were mass uprisings against Communist rule in Poland
and an attempt to overthrow the Communist regime in Hungary, which
was suppressed by the Soviet army after bloody street fighting.

Hungarian Uprising

In 1956, what began as a student-led protest against the Soviet-backed
Hungarian People's Republic erupted into a nationwide revolt against the
communist regime as Hungary vowed to disengage from the Warsaw Pact.
Known as the **Hungarian Uprising**, the revolt took hold quickly and the
government collapsed. After initially claiming their willingness to nego-
tiate, the Soviets crushed the uprising, killing 2,500 Hungarians; 200,000
more fled as refugees.

The Cultural "Thaw"

Three waves of cultural "Thaw" continued the process of de-Stalinization in 1953, 1956, and 1962. A 1954 novel entitled *Thaw* by Ilya Ehrenburg signaled a liberalization in literature and film, which notably included the publication of Alexander Solzhenitsyn's novella *A Day in the Life of Ivan Denisovich* in 1962, the story of a prison camp inmate. With much stopping and starting, these waves would often be replaced by conservative attacks, as repressive measures were still common. For example, religion was prosecuted once again and thousands of churches shut down.

A campaign was waged against "idleness" that targeted individuals without official employment, including artists who were not members of the state-led unions, such as the poet Joseph Brodsky. In 1957, Boris Pasternak was persecuted because of the publication in the West of his novel *Doctor Zhivago*.

Society and Economy Under Khrushchev

During this time, ordinary people were not necessarily better off than they had been before the war. There was gradually increased attention paid to consumer goods, but the greatest push was made to provide desperately needed housing, in the form of cheap, mass-produced apartment buildings. Collective farmers were stripped of most of their private plots and food prices rose. Mass protests resulted, but were hushed up. In Novocherkassk in 1962, protestors were shot by the army.

In spite of the challenges people faced under the new regime, Khrushchev's de-Stalinization efforts were successful. Soon after Stalin died, his influence diminished; he was mentioned less often in newspapers, and his pictures, busts, and other images were removed. In 1961, Stalingrad, the city that had been renamed from Tsaritsyn in honor of Stalin in 1925, was renamed Volgograd.

Soviet Relations with the U.S. Under Khrushchev

"Peaceful Coexistence" and the Space Race

Khrushchev pursued a policy of "peaceful coexistence" with the West after the end of the Korean War, based in part on the reality that nuclear arsenals on both sides meant "Mutually Assured Destruction" (MAD) would be the inevitable result of a direct military confrontation. The Cold War in this era was fought through the "space race," in which both sides sought to demonstrate their technical prowess and achieve parity in missiles and nuclear warheads. Until the 1960s, the Soviet Union had the capacity to destroy Europe but not really to reach the United States. But in 1957, when the Soviets launched the first satellite into space, **Sputnik**, they also demonstrated their ability to reach the U.S. with ICBMs (Inter-Continental Ballistic Missiles) and greatly reduced their conventional army. In 1961, Soviet cosmonaut **Yury Gagarin** became the first man in space, urging the U.S. to intensify its efforts in the same realm.

The Cold War in Europe Under Khrushchev

The **Warsaw Pact**, the Soviet counter to NATO (North Atlantic Treaty Organization), was created in 1955 to formalize Soviet dominance of the Eastern bloc. In 1959, Khrushchev visited the United States, putting on a show of one-upmanship but basically warming relations. However, in 1960, a United States U-2 spy plane was shot down over Russia, renewing tensions. In 1961, the German Democratic Republic began construction of the Berlin Wall, separating NATO-controlled West Berlin and Communist-controlled East Berlin and surrounding East Germany.

The Cuban Missile Crisis

Then, in 1962, Khrushchev secretly moved nuclear-tipped missiles to Cuba, ruled by Fidel Castro. His reasons are not entirely clear, but the move seems to have been intended to protect Castro's regime from an imminent U.S. invasion and to push the U.S. to remove its own nuclear missiles from Turkey. The U.S. detected the move late and declared a "quarantine," in effect a blockade that could be interpreted as an act of war. This stand-off was the closest the world has come to a massive nuclear war, but Khrushchev and President Kennedy never stopped talking to each other through the crisis, and it is clear that neither wanted to risk MAD. In the end, the USSR removed its missiles from Cuba and the U.S. agreed not to invade, as well as to remove its missiles from Turkey. However, this last provision was kept secret, making the outcome look like a Soviet defeat.

Proxy Wars

A proxy war is a conflict between major powers in which neither power fights the other directly. Rather, smaller countries fight on behalf of the major powers, who provide support through the supply of arms, equipment, military training, financial aid, and at times, military troops. During the Cold War, proxy wars served as a way for the United States and USSR to maintain their respective spheres of influence without getting into a direct conflict, which held the threat of nuclear war. Perhaps the most well-known proxy war during Khrushchev's leadership in the USSR is the **Second Indochina War**, also known as the **Vietnam War** (1955–1975).

The Suez Crisis

In July 1956, supported by Soviet funds, Egyptian President Gamal Abdel Nasser nationalized the Suez Canal, prohibiting its use by Israel. Israel, backed by the British and the French, launched an attack to retake the canal. Khrushchev, preoccupied with the Hungarian Uprising, threatened to launch a nuclear attack against the three nations if they did not withdraw and stop their offensive. President Eisenhower warned Khrushchev against such threatening rhetoric but also threatened the British, French, and Israelis with economic sanctions if they did not stop their offensive. Ultimately, the British and French withdrew in December and the Israelis, feeling pressure from the United States, withdrew the following March.

Rift with China

In 1960–1961, the USSR split with Communist China, a rift that persisted until 1989. **Mao Zedong** did not want to support or participate in Khrushchev's policy of "peaceful coexistence" with the West, nor did he approve of de-Stalinization. Chinese Communists viewed the USSR as revisionist traitors to the cause and unworthy of trust. The result was a kind of second Cold War between China and the Soviet Union, in which China built its own system of allies in Asia and Africa. The long-term effect of the rift was to alter the global power structure based in third-world allies and satellites in ways that did not favor Soviet interests.

THE BREZHNEV ERA

Khrushchev's successor, **Leonid Brezhnev**, ruled the Soviet Union from 1964–1982. This period came to be popularly known as "stagnation," referring to the sense of political and social stability, but also a slow-down in the growth of the Soviet economy.

Growth and Stagnation

In October 1964, Nikita Khrushchev was removed from power in a bloodless coup organized by the KGB. His position went to Leonid Brezhnev, who represented a younger generation untainted by direct participation in the Stalinist terror (though many had reached their positions by replacing purge victims).

Brezhnev's style of rule was very different from Khrushchev and Stalin: he reintroduced Lenin's earlier practice of "collective leadership," that is, of sharing power with a small group of senior Communists known as the **Politburo**.

Society and Economy During "Stagnation"

Although the Brezhnev period was marked by a slowdown in economic growth, at the same time, it was a period of social stability and a much higher standard of living for ordinary Soviet citizens. Successes in space exploration, aviation, nuclear energy, education, medical care and social services, arts and sciences, and sports created the impression of a stabilized regime after decades of upheaval. Under Brezhnev, Soviet citizens enjoyed free education, free basic healthcare, and very low housing costs.

In addition, the state invested in large-scale, long-term capital investment and infrastructure projects, such as housing, subways, and the complete electrification of rural villages.

In the 1970s, the Soviet Union finally acquired unified transportation and energy networks, and the government sponsored massive irrigation and reforestation programs.

Soviet Vulnerabilities

At the same time, the economy had become dependent on the export of raw materials, especially oil and gas after the 1973 oil crisis. Many high-tech industries such as electronics were not developing, and labor productivity was not high enough to compete with other major economies. Consumer goods were often of low quality and still insufficient to meet demand. Agriculture had been deprived of resources for so long that the USSR was forced to purchase grain abroad. People were eating better than in turbulent previous decades, but it was still not enough. Private garden plots were again allowed, and there were occasional attempts to introduce limited elements of the market, with the intention of making state-owned businesses accountable and profitable. Government effort was directed toward culture and leisure, but what developed instead was a working-class urban culture that led to frequent mass riots, usually aimed at police and the courts. These were not mentioned in the press, and rampant alcoholism and violent crime were similarly ignored. After 1969, modern terrorism began to affect the Soviet Union, with recurring plane hijackings and suicide bombings.

Ideological Dissent

Soon after Brezhnev came to power, the policies of Thaw were abandoned, to be replaced with a cult of the "Great Patriotic War." Stalin was rehabilitated in a limited way, mentioned as part of the story of Soviet growth and victory in World War II, but not glorified. Ideological dissenters were persecuted, as in the 1965 trial of two writers, Siniavsky and Daniel, who had published abroad works that were censored in the Soviet Union. They were sentenced to prison amid public protests. Czech socialists rose up in the **Prague Spring of 1968** and were suppressed by tanks sent from Moscow to prop up the local regime. Human rights activists in the Soviet bloc were also harassed. But overall, the scale of dissent was small, involving relatively isolated intellectuals without broad social support.

Dissidents' Beliefs and Practices

The overwhelming majority of dissidents were actually pro-Soviet: they wanted to reform the Soviet system but leave its foundations untouched. Rather than another revolution, they hoped to hold the regime accountable to its official promises of justice and liberation. These protests were nonviolent and insisted on observing existing state law. They varied ideologically, with some emphasizing Communism, others western liberalism, and still others nationalist themes (Russian or other). Finally, there was religious dissent, including nonconforming Orthodox believers and other confessions or sects.

Official Persecution of Dissent

Dissidents were punished with imprisonment; forced commitment to psychiatric wards; and, for the most famous cultural figures, forced emigration from the USSR. Joseph Brodsky emigrated in 1972, and Alexander Solzhenitsyn published *The Gulag Archipelago* abroad in 1973 and emigrated in 1974. Andrei Sakharov (1921–1989), a nuclear physicist who became a human rights activist, was sentenced to internal exile from 1980 until 1986, when he was allowed to return to his home in Moscow.

TIP: Andrei Sakharov was awarded the Nobel Peace Prize in 1975.

Détente

Brezhnev created good working relationships with Western leaders, with the intention of preventing another Cuban Missile Crisis. The Soyuz-Apollo joint space mission beginning in 1967 reduced the antagonism of the space race, and a series of agreements in the 1970s reduced the risk of a major nuclear war. These included:

- The **Soviet-West German treaty**, 1970
- The **ABM and SALT-1 disarmament treaties**, 1972
- **Nixon's visit to Moscow**, 1972
- **Brezhnev's visit to the United States**, 1973
- The **Helsinki agreements** confirming European borders, economic cooperation, and human rights pledges
- The **SALT-2 disarmament treaty** signed in Vienna

Cultural and economic contacts also began to be encouraged within limits, as when Pepsi was brought to the USSR. At the same time, the Soviet Union continued to improve its armaments, reaching strategic nuclear parity with the U.S. and creating a powerful navy and air force. Détente ended in December 1979 with the Soviet invasion of Afghanistan.

Proxy Wars in the Third World

Despite détente, the USSR had intensified its efforts in the Third World under Brezhnev. In early 1965, the Soviets provided massive aid to North Vietnam and actively cooperated with China. Few Soviet soldiers were directly involved in the fighting and generally worked only as military advisers and technical specialists. In addition, the USSR supported communist governments fighting civil wars against rebels supported by the U.S. or other western powers, as in Ethiopia after 1974, Angola after 1975, and Nicaragua beginning in 1981 (supporting the Sandinistas, who were militarily successful but agreed to a political compromise in 1988). In the Near East, the USSR provided massive aid to Egypt and Syria in the Arab-Israeli wars of 1967, 1973, and 1982, without success. In other areas, the Soviets supported Communist rebels or governments that were overthrown by pro-American forces, such as the Chilean socialist democratic government overthrown in 1973.

War in Afghanistan

The 1978 April Revolution in Afghanistan established a left-wing republic. The new government's social reforms were resisted by an Islamic opposition financed by the United States, resulting in a civil war. The Afghan government called for Soviet troops. The Kremlin at first declined, but changed its mind when Hafizullah Amin seized power in September 1979. Amin was seen as an unreliable and cruel dictator who launched mass executions, and the USSR feared that Amin would either defect to the U.S. or bring about the defeat of communism in Afghanistan. They therefore used Amin's own request for troops to overthrow him. Soviet troops seized key points in Afghanistan, killed Amin, and replaced him with the more moderate Babrak Karmal. However, the USSR had no plan for what to do next, including the potential for actual warfare, since it was assumed they would withdraw. But from the start, they engaged in open fighting with Islamists. The Soviets' heavily armed troops won the initial full-scale battles but after 1983 became beleaguered by ongoing guerilla warfare and terrorist attacks.

REFORM AND COLLAPSE

In the early 1980s, the Soviet Union was facing increased pressures abroad and a series of economic problems at home; however, none of these indicated its imminent fall. Mikhail Gorbachev was brought to power by his Politburo colleagues in 1985 with the expectation of a modest program of reforms, but within only a couple of years, Soviet ideology and the Communist Party's political control crumbled, and Gorbachev unexpectedly lost his predominance to Boris Yeltsin, who became the first president of the independent Russian Federation.

Global Challengers and the End of Détente

With the election of Margaret Thatcher as Prime Minister of the UK in 1979 and of Ronald Reagan as U.S. President in 1980, détente was abandoned by the West, with Soviet actions in Afghanistan as the excuse. Both leaders were strongly ideological in their opposition to the Soviet Union, and they became swayed by intelligence reports that Soviet military capabilities were greater than they probably were, as well as by theories that increased military spending on their part could push the Soviet Union, in its efforts to respond, to collapse (this remains a popular theory to explain the eventual collapse, though there is little evidence to support it).

....

TIP: Pope John Paul II (elected 1978) was of Polish origin, and during his pastoral trips to Poland tacitly encouraged its anti-Communist Solidarity movement, although the latter's—and the Pope's—role in ending Communism is usually greatly exaggerated.

....

Pressure Against the USSR

Western pressure was applied in various ways. In 1980, most Western countries boycotted the Olympic Games in Moscow (in return, the USSR boycotted the 1984 Games in Los Angeles). In 1983, a Soviet airplane mistakenly shot down Korean Air Lines Flight 007 that had strayed over a restricted military area, thinking it to be a spy plane. President Reagan responded with a media campaign accusing the USSR of a "crime against humanity." Finally, the U.S. began to deploy intermediate-range Pershing II missiles to Europe, hoping to gain an advantage in nuclear arms. In a series of speeches, including one in 1983 that referred to the USSR as an "**evil empire**" living in "totalitarian darkness," Reagan called for an aggressive anti-Soviet strategy. Finally, the Soviet Union was sharply criticized for its poor human rights record.

Soviet Reaction

Soviet leaders in the early 1980s were of course aware of these challenges, but they thought Reagan to be a dangerous fanatic and were determined to invest in more advanced weapons to counter his threats (although this cannot be seen as an increase in Soviet spending on the military, since military spending was maximized almost throughout the Soviet period). The nonviolent "soft power" threat, however, could not be as easily addressed, and the exposure of Soviet human rights abuses did take a toll on the USSR's reputation and bargaining power.

External Factors (Afghanistan, Islam)

Because their troops had been invited in, the Soviets considered Afghanistan to be an internal Communist matter, like Prague in 1968, but the West portrayed the Soviet entry into Afghanistan as an unprovoked invasion and used it as an excuse to end détente. The West then imposed economic sanctions, although they were ineffective because Europeans did not fully participate. The U.S. had provided the Afghan mujahedeen with advanced weapons, only a few months before the Soviet invasion in 1979, including Stinger missiles.

Soviet Escalation and Withdrawal

The USSR in reply combined large-scale army operations with Special Forces raids to intercept weapon supplies smuggled from Pakistan. The Soviets were militarily successful, but, having from the start planned for a limited engagement, they were anxious to pull out. Large-scale fighting with significant casualties was deeply unpopular, but the Soviets could not find a political solution. Gorbachev's initial solution in 1985–1987 was not to pull out but actually to intensify warfare. Only in 1988, as part of the **Geneva Agreements**, did the USSR promise to pull out of Afghanistan while the U.S. and Pakistan promised to stop supporting the mujahedeen. The Soviet army pulled out by February 1989, but continued to support the regime, and the Americans and Pakistan continued to support the mujahedeen. The results of the conflict were inconclusive; instability in the region made Islamic terrorism a continuing problem as the population had been antagonized by external forces, but the effort was a military success as they were able to maintain the USSR's own safe borders while it lasted. Immediately after Soviet withdrawal, Islamist fighters started penetrating into Soviet Central Asia.

Perestroika and Glasnost

In March 1985, Mikhail Gorbachev came to power, representing a younger generation educated in less chaotic and more idealistic circumstances than Brezhnev and his peers. However, for the first two years of his rule, no changes were made, although many Brezhnev-era bureaucrats were replaced with younger men during that period.

In January 1987, the Party announced a new policy of perestroika (restructuring) to be the official state doctrine. The policy dictated that the USSR would remain socialist, but the aim was to return to "Leninist norms," a rather idealized vision of the Party's first principles. Following a period of falling oil prices and the **Chernobyl nuclear disaster** in 1986, a limited economic liberalization was begun, allowing private business and trade (euphemistically called "cooperatives") to operate, especially after Gorbachev's Law on Cooperatives of 1988 that allowed the use of hired labor. Private trade and small-scale manufacture grew rapidly but did not produce the expected economic miracle. To the contrary, existing supply networks were disrupted and periodic shortages of staple consumer goods became common in 1987–1988. Additionally, Armenia suffered a devastating earthquake in Spitak in 1988, which exposed the inability of the Soviet government to financially support its satellite nations.

Another element of the new direction was glasnost (openness), which meant the relaxation of censorship on all levels. The government allowed previously prohibited works of literature to be published, including the incendiary works of Solzhenitsyn about the GULAG system. It also allowed public discussion of such problematic topics as the legacy of Stalinism, prostitution, drug problems, and more. Religious practice became completely unrestricted, and all dissidents were freed.

Aside from the economic and cultural liberalization, another key element of Gorbachev's reforms was to permit open political dialogue for the first time in Soviet history. The **19th Party Conference** in 1988 included delegates who were not appointed from above, and it decided that free elections to local councils (Soviets) would be held everywhere from then on. Finally, the first **Congress of People's Deputies** was convened in 1989, with many non-Communists elected as deputies. Sharp discussions at the Congress were televised, showing that the Party's monopoly on political life was coming to an end and exposing viewers to alternative points of view.

In foreign policy, Gorbachev at first sought to bargain with the West on equal terms and to recreate the détente of the 1970s, but he met resistance from Reagan and Thatcher, who rejected most of his arms control proposals. But after 1987, Gorbachev began to make significant and mostly one-sided concessions to the U.S., beginning with a treaty liquidating short- and intermediate-range missiles.

Reemergence of the Nationalities Issues

The power struggle in the Kremlin combined with, and in some cases rekindled, longstanding ethnic tensions and damaged the image of the USSR as a land where numerous national groups could live in peace and harmony. For instance, in 1986, there were anti-Russian riots in Kazakhstan. In 1987, the conflict between Armenians and the Azeri over the region of Nagorno-Karabakh (mostly populated by Armenians but administratively part of Azerbaijan) grew into open warfare using weapons stolen from Soviet police and the military. In 1988–1990, this conflict spilled into bloody pogroms against the large Armenian minority in Baku, Sumgait (Sumqayit), and other Azeri cities.

Time and again, Gorbachev sent additional troops to stop the fighting but was unable or unwilling to address the underlying causes. Mostly nonviolent nationalistic movements also developed in the Baltic republics, advocating for their autonomy and eventual independence. These were tolerated because they were officially formed to support Gorbachev and his reforms. By the time Gorbachev realized the danger and ordered his troops to suppress the separatists early in 1991, it was too late to have any effect.

Finally, Gorbachev's position was seriously undermined in 1990 by the election of **Boris Yeltsin** as the leader of the Russian Federation. The Russian Federation was the largest Union republic that had not had its own political identity throughout the Soviet period, even though it included most of Soviet population and economic resources. Yeltsin was determined to create his own power structure and to overcome Gorbachev by destroying the Soviet Union in the process, if necessary.

Revolutions in Eastern Europe

In 1989, Communist regimes fell throughout Soviet satellite states in Eastern Europe, including Poland, Hungary, East Germany, Czechoslovakia, Romania, and Bulgaria. This happened in part because Gorbachev's government felt that it did not have the moral and military-financial resources to maintain Soviet control (because it wanted to improve relations with the West) and also because Gorbachev felt that conservative Communist leaders in Eastern Europe were resisting introducing their own versions of perestroika, thinking that he and his policies would be short-lived. Gorbachev in effect ruled out the possibility that the USSR would support Communist regimes with military force if necessary.

The "Velvet" Revolution and the Fall of the Berlin Wall

As a result, on April 4, 1989, the Polish government legalized the anti-Communist Solidarity movement and permitted free elections. A similar process took place in Bulgaria and in Hungary, which permitted non-Communist parties and began to dismantle its fortified border with Austria. Czechoslovakia opened its borders and refused to forcefully quell protests, resulting in the "Velvet Revolution," ending Communist rule with the installation of a new president, **Václav Havel**.

In the fall of 1989, East Germany's leader **Erich Honecker** faced mass protests from East Germans who wanted to leave the country. Honecker attempted to resist these pressures but eventually gave in to public protests and resigned on October 18, 1989. The nonviolent protests and growing numbers of East German refugees leaving the country continued until, at a press conference on November 9, the announcement was made that official border crossings through the Berlin Wall into West Berlin were open.

People began tearing off pieces of the Wall to keep as souvenirs and creating unofficial border crossings. On June 13, 1990, the East German military began the official dismantling of the Berlin Wall. By August 1, 1990, most of the roads connecting East and West Berlin that had been severed by the Wall had been rebuilt and reopened.

TIP: Although the fall of the Berlin Wall marked the beginning of the reunification of Germany, the official reunification happened on October 3, 1990, with the dissolution of East Germany.

Violence in Romania and the End of the Warsaw Pact

The only country in Eastern Europe where the fall of Communism involved considerable violence was Romania, whose dictator, Nicolae Ceauçescu, was determined to hold on to his power; he eventually faced the defection of his troops and was murdered with his wife Elena. Gorbachev refused to intervene in any of these events, and, on July 1, 1991, the Warsaw Pact was officially dissolved.

End of the Union of Soviet Socialist Republics

During 1989, as Gorbachev's regime gave up its control of Eastern Europe and was facing political dissent, separatist movements, and ethnic tensions on its own territory, the future fate of the Soviet Union came into question. Gorbachev's plan, shared by many in the leadership, was to revive the USSR by drafting a looser, more democratic Union treaty that would provide greater autonomy for the constituent republics.

A referendum on the future of the Soviet Union was held on March 17, 1991. Separatist authorities in Georgia, Moldavia (Moldova), and the Baltic republics refused to participate, although their citizens could still vote with the assistance of USSR officials. In the Baltic republics, especially, their large Russian minorities (up to 40 percent overwhelmingly voted against independence. Votes in favor of preserving the union were also very high in Azerbaijan and in Central Asian republics (over 90 percent), and even in Ukraine (over 80 percent). Overall, almost 78 percent of the vote was in favor of keeping a renewed version of the USSR. The new Union treaty was scheduled to be signed on August 20, 1991.

The Coup Attempt in August 1991

A number of key Soviet officials believed that the new treaty would amount to a breakup of the USSR and would violate the popular will expressed in the March referendum. They formed a conspiracy to introduce a state of emergency and remove from power secession-minded figures, especially Boris Yeltsin. It is unclear how much Gorbachev knew about the proposed coup or whether he approved.

The coup began on August 18 when Gorbachev was vacationing in Crimea and the public was told that he was sick. Gorbachev claimed that he was put under house arrest. Coup leaders brought large numbers of loyal troops into Moscow, but they quickly lost their nerve and refused to take more decisive and violent measures, especially against Boris Yeltsin, who was barricaded in his headquarters, known as the White House. By August 21, the troops were ordered out and the coup leaders surrendered (but were eventually pardoned).

Dissolution of the Soviet Union

The failed coup made it politically impossible to revive the Soviet Union under its own name and Gorbachev quickly lost whatever remained of his power. On December 8, 1991, Boris Yeltsin met with leaders of Ukraine and Belorussia, known as the **Belavezha Accords**, without Gorbachev's knowledge, and agreed to formally dissolve the Soviet Union and to replace it with a loose alliance known as the Commonwealth of Independent States.

Causes of the Soviet Collapse

The collapse of the Soviet Union, though it came suddenly and surprised many observers, can now be seen to have had deep roots in a wide variety of irresolvable conflicts and challenges, in which foreign policy disasters and competition with the West played a relatively minor role.

Recognized factors destabilizing the Soviet regime include the following:

- The centralized economy was overextended and inflexible after over-investment in heavy industry in the early Brezhnev years.
- Soviet science education was compartmentalized and overly technical, impeding the development of technological innovation and problem-solving and contributing to disasters such as the Chernobyl nuclear meltdown.
- The maintenance of the Soviet bloc had become an economic and political liability.

- Increased reliance on oil and gas exports made the Soviet Union economically dependent on complicated conflicts in the Middle East.
- The Brezhnev-era leadership was riven with corruption and embedded in organized crime rings.
- Marxist ideology had lost its grip on ordinary people, who had sacrificed a great deal for the promise of socialist equality and liberation only to see corrupt officials continue to ignore or suppress the demands of ordinary workers, while the publications released under glasnost made people mistrustful of anything coming from the government.
- The development of nationalist movements in several parts of the Soviet Union challenged the center's overall ideological and political control and led to violence and separatist pressures.
- Increased access to information through the spread of television and eventually the lessening of censorship highlighted unflattering comparisons with the West, which made people dissatisfied with the state's weak attempts to meet demand in consumer goods and standards of living.
- Increased media attention on Brezhnev and his leadership in their later years made them appear out of touch, weak, and ridiculous.
- Reagan's decision to use the arms reduction talks of the 1980s to publicly hold the USSR accountable for human rights abuses according to the terms of the 1975 Helsinki Accords created international pressure, at a time of military and diplomatic embarrassments.

On the whole, while the USSR's inability to compete with the West on a wide range of fronts was a major factor in its collapse, this inability was due to problems long pre-dating Reagan's election and may not have been decisive in itself. It was the combination of these factors with serious internal instabilities and the disaffection of the Soviet population with its own regime that resulted in the total lack of support for either the coup leaders or for Gorbachev in August 1991, and the relative openness on the part of sufficient numbers of people (though not a majority) for the nation-based breakup of republics represented by Yeltsin and fulfilled by the formation of the Commonwealth of Independent States.

Gorbachev's Legacy

Mikhail Gorbachev has been much lauded in the West since the collapse of the Soviet Union. He is credited with eliminating the most oppressive aspects of Soviet rule and helping to bring about a relatively bloodless end to the Cold War and the Soviet Communist experiment, in the process opening the Russian Federation and other newly independent states to the global marketplace (which was expected to bring prosperity to the region, though that has not been the case).

Within Russia, Gorbachev's leadership is viewed as a failure that lost Russia its position as a great power, as the second largest economy in the world, and as a stable social system with a functioning safety net for its most vulnerable citizens. Meanwhile, some foreign policy observers have noted that the Cold War was also a long period of relative peace, when major warfare was avoided.

Gorbachev's legacy is mixed: the roots of collapse were deep, pre-dating his rise and thus making it doubtful that he could have done anything to prevent it. Several former Soviet satellite states in Eastern Europe, such as Poland and the Czech Republic, have developed into peaceful and relatively prosperous democracies. Yet the consequences of Communist collapse have been costly for many people of the former Soviet Union and some of its satellites. Regional conflicts there and in the Middle East have emerged or intensified since the Soviet collapse, often fueled by competing nationalist movements, resurgent right-wing politics, and/or competition over oil and gas resources. Authoritarian successor regimes have replaced Soviet power in many places, displaying many of the worst aspects of the Communist Party. Post-Soviet leaders in Russia and other successor states have also presided over economic systems as deeply corrupt as ever but lacking the relative stability and safety net provided under late Communism; enormous wealth has been amassed by a few, while the economic circumstances of most people remain shaky and rocked by frequent crises.

SUMMING IT UP

- Today's **Russia rose to power in the late fifteenth century,** when Muscovy grew to become the largest state in Europe and eventually in the world. Tsar Peter the Great changed Russia's politics and culture and adopted the title of "emperor" to assert his dominance.
- In the early twentieth century Russia was the only major European state ruled by an **autocracy** (under Nicholas II). During the Revolution of 1905–1907, Nicholas II was persuaded to establish the **State Duma**, which could control the budget and grant basic civil rights. The **Russian Orthodox Church** remained Russia's state religion.
- **Russia's economy in the early twentieth century was one of the largest in the world** due to agriculture. Still, per capita incomes remained among the lowest in Europe.

- **Industrial enterprises** appeared in Russia in the seventeenth century, and Peter the Great made an effort to establish a metalworking industry in the Ural Mountains. Russia's rail network was the largest in Europe in 1914—the Trans-Siberian Railroad connected European Russia to the Pacific Ocean. Russia's financial system improved with the introduction of the gold standard in 1897.
- Until the **Emancipation of 1861**, almost half of all peasants were enserfed. After, noble landowners lost some of their land but generally retained their wealth, access to education and state service, and power in the government. At this time, there was a growing middle class that included merchants, entrepreneurs, and various professionals.
- **Russia was among the victors at the Congress of Vienna** but lost the Crimean War, which facilitated the wars of German Unification. The rise of a powerful Germany led to an alliance with France in 1893. At this time, Russia was also engaged in the Great Game with Great Britain and came into conflict with Japan in 1904–1905.
- The **populist movement** was widespread in the 1860s and 1870s. Populists sought to achieve social transformation by working through the common people; some turned to terror to force the government to make concessions. Tsar Alexander II was hunted down and assassinated in 1881. Populists were still very influential in Russia, forming the Socialist Revolutionary Party in 1914.
- In 1903, the leading Marxist party, the **Social Democrats**, split into two parties: the **Bolsheviks** (led by Vladimir Lenin) and the **Mensheviks** (led by Yulii Martov. By 1914, Marxist leaders like Lenin and Leon Trotsky had fallen out of favor and gone into hiding, and others, including Joseph Stalin, had been arrested.
- **Russia entered the First World War on the side of Great Britain and France to protect Serbia**, but by 1918 Russia's empire had collapsed as a result of not being able to withstand the costs of the war. Following the collapse, the Bolsheviks reemerged to seize power and overthrow the tsarist government during the 1917 revolutions. The February/March Revolution of 1917 forced Nicholas II to step down. The October Revolution that year brought the Bolsheviks to power. The Romanov family was later executed by Bolshevik operatives.
- Under the Bolsheviks and Lenin, Russia adopted a policy of **war communism**, which included complete control over the economy (seizing all banks and deposits, nationalizing all large industries, banning private entrepreneurship, and assuming total control over food supplies and trade). The fallout from these policies led to out-of-control inflation, a massive black market, and eventually a famine that claimed 5 million lives. Despite this, the Bolsheviks maintained control after a civil war with the Cossacks.

- Russia formally became the **Union of Soviet Socialist Republics** (USSR, Soviet Union) in 1922, with power over the republics held by the Red Army and the Communist Party.
- After Lenin's death, **Joseph Stalin** emerged as the new leader of the USSR. He began to implement state-controlled collective farms to replace private farms that were unable (or unwilling) to keep up with the state's food and export needs. The poor organization of these farms, coupled with environmental factors, led to the Great Famine in 1931–1932, during which 2–8 million people died and more than 40 million people suffered.
- Stalin's **First Five-Year Plan (1928–1932)** was intended to modernize the USSR's infrastructure, energy plants, raw materials processing, and machine-building plants. Industrial production grew rapidly (leaving the USSR second only to the U.S.), but unrealistic goals and faked statistics undermined the program's success.
- The **cultural revolution** established state-sponsorship of art, film, literature and music and theater and encouraged literacy. It created a boom in the arts, but was also used to circulate anti-religion/pro-Stalinist-government propaganda.
- **In the Second World War, the Soviet Union eventually joined the Allied Powers** against Germany, breaking the Soviet-German Nonaggression Treaty and ending a long period of diplomatic isolation. After the war, Russia received Eastern and Southeastern European territories that were formerly under German control.
- After the war, Stalin's regime instituted a strict program of **Russian and Communist nationalism**, backed by force and propaganda. Conflicts over USSR territory formed the basis of the Cold War with the U.S. and western European nations.
- Stalin's successor, **Nikita Khrushchev**, reinforced the Soviet regime and introduced a cultural "Thaw," though repressive force was still common. Khrushchev sought diplomacy with the West in the 1950s, while introducing the concept of "Mutually Assured Destruction" (MAD) as a consequence for military confrontation with Western nations.
- The USSR also invested heavily in the "**space race**," with cosmonaut **Yuri Gagarin** becoming the first man in space.
- The **Cuban Missile Crisis of 1962** was caused by Khrushchev sending nuclear missiles to Cuba. The threat of MAD led to an agreement between Khrushchev and U.S. President John F. Kennedy, though the Cold War would continue until 1989.
- Khrushchev's successor, **Leonid Brezhnev**, presided over "stagnation" as the Soviet Union's economic growth slowed. He also presided over "détente," or improved diplomatic relations with Western nations.

- **Détente ended under Mikhail Gorbachev's regime** when UK prime minister Margaret Thatcher and U.S. president Ronald Reagan came to power, as they were ideologically opposed to the USSR.
- **After a failed coup in 1989** that was supposed to maintain central USSR control over its republics, **Boris Yeltsin**, Gorbachev's successor, **agreed to formally dissolve the USSR into independent states**. Among the primary factors for this were the Soviet Union's collapsing nationalized industries and the USSR's inability to compete with the United States.

Chapter 4

History of the Soviet Union Post-Test

POST-TEST ANSWER SHEET

21. Ⓐ Ⓑ Ⓒ Ⓓ	37. Ⓐ Ⓑ Ⓒ Ⓓ	53. Ⓐ Ⓑ Ⓒ Ⓓ
22. Ⓐ Ⓑ Ⓒ Ⓓ	38. Ⓐ Ⓑ Ⓒ Ⓓ	54. Ⓐ Ⓑ Ⓒ Ⓓ
23. Ⓐ Ⓑ Ⓒ Ⓓ	39. Ⓐ Ⓑ Ⓒ Ⓓ	55. Ⓐ Ⓑ Ⓒ Ⓓ
24. Ⓐ Ⓑ Ⓒ Ⓓ	40. Ⓐ Ⓑ Ⓒ Ⓓ	56. Ⓐ Ⓑ Ⓒ Ⓓ
25. Ⓐ Ⓑ Ⓒ Ⓓ	41. Ⓐ Ⓑ Ⓒ Ⓓ	57. Ⓐ Ⓑ Ⓒ Ⓓ
26. Ⓐ Ⓑ Ⓒ Ⓓ	42. Ⓐ Ⓑ Ⓒ Ⓓ	58. Ⓐ Ⓑ Ⓒ Ⓓ
27. Ⓐ Ⓑ Ⓒ Ⓓ	43. Ⓐ Ⓑ Ⓒ Ⓓ	59. Ⓐ Ⓑ Ⓒ Ⓓ
28. Ⓐ Ⓑ Ⓒ Ⓓ	44. Ⓐ Ⓑ Ⓒ Ⓓ	60. Ⓐ Ⓑ Ⓒ Ⓓ
29. Ⓐ Ⓑ Ⓒ Ⓓ	45. Ⓐ Ⓑ Ⓒ Ⓓ	61. Ⓐ Ⓑ Ⓒ Ⓓ
30. Ⓐ Ⓑ Ⓒ Ⓓ	46. Ⓐ Ⓑ Ⓒ Ⓓ	62. Ⓐ Ⓑ Ⓒ Ⓓ
31. Ⓐ Ⓑ Ⓒ Ⓓ	47. Ⓐ Ⓑ Ⓒ Ⓓ	63. Ⓐ Ⓑ Ⓒ Ⓓ
32. Ⓐ Ⓑ Ⓒ Ⓓ	48. Ⓐ Ⓑ Ⓒ Ⓓ	64. Ⓐ Ⓑ Ⓒ Ⓓ
33. Ⓐ Ⓑ Ⓒ Ⓓ	49. Ⓐ Ⓑ Ⓒ Ⓓ	65. Ⓐ Ⓑ Ⓒ Ⓓ
34. Ⓐ Ⓑ Ⓒ Ⓓ	50. Ⓐ Ⓑ Ⓒ Ⓓ	66. Ⓐ Ⓑ Ⓒ Ⓓ
35. Ⓐ Ⓑ Ⓒ Ⓓ	51. Ⓐ Ⓑ Ⓒ Ⓓ	67. Ⓐ Ⓑ Ⓒ Ⓓ
36. Ⓐ Ⓑ Ⓒ Ⓓ	52. Ⓐ Ⓑ Ⓒ Ⓓ	68. Ⓐ Ⓑ Ⓒ Ⓓ

69. Ⓐ Ⓑ Ⓒ Ⓓ   **73.** Ⓐ Ⓑ Ⓒ Ⓓ   **77.** Ⓐ Ⓑ Ⓒ Ⓓ

70. Ⓐ Ⓑ Ⓒ Ⓓ   **74.** Ⓐ Ⓑ Ⓒ Ⓓ   **78.** Ⓐ Ⓑ Ⓒ Ⓓ

71. Ⓐ Ⓑ Ⓒ Ⓓ   **75.** Ⓐ Ⓑ Ⓒ Ⓓ   **79.** Ⓐ Ⓑ Ⓒ Ⓓ

72. Ⓐ Ⓑ Ⓒ Ⓓ   **76.** Ⓐ Ⓑ Ⓒ Ⓓ   **80.** Ⓐ Ⓑ Ⓒ Ⓓ

HISTORY OF THE SOVIET UNION POST-TEST

Directions: Carefully read each of the following 60 questions. Choose the best answer to each question and fill in the corresponding circle on the answer sheet. The Answer Key and Explanations can be found following this post-test.

1. What happened to Soviet territory in Europe as a result of the Second World War?

   A. The USSR received part of Eastern Prussia and kept the lands it annexed in 1939–1940.
   B. The USSR annexed Finland and Denmark as the Scandinavian Soviet Socialist Republic.
   C. The USSR took parts of German territory but restored independence to the Baltic states.
   D. The USSR directly incorporated East Berlin as an exclave of the Russian Federation.

2. Which of the following was NOT one of the Great Reforms of the 1860s?

   A. Serf emancipation
   B. Judicial reform
   C. Freedom of speech
   D. Local self-government

3. What happened to Leningrad in 1941–1944?

   A. It was besieged and much of its population starved to death, but it was never captured.
   B. It was captured by the German Army and its large Jewish population murdered.
   C. It served as a temporary capital of the USSR despite the danger of being captured.
   D. It became known as Tankograd because Soviet tank factories were evacuated there.

4. What happened to Russia's industrial production in the 1890s?

    A. Growth was limited to textiles and food processing.

    B. Growth was most notable in heavy industry and railroad construction.

    C. Industry stagnated because it could not face competition from Germany.

    D. Industry declined because Old Believer merchants opposed capitalism.

5. Russia's performance during the First World War suffered because of a lack of

    A. industrial capacity leading to munitions shortages.

    B. sufficient manpower to make up for battle casualties.

    C. naval power, such as submarines and battleships.

    D. powerful fortresses to protect western borders.

6. The February Revolution of 1917 started when

    A. the German threat to Petrograd induced the Duma to call for emergency laws.

    B. the assassination of Rasputin started anti-clerical demonstrations in Petrograd.

    C. interruptions of the food supply in Petrograd led to strikes and riots by workers.

    D. the Socialist-led Petrograd garrison demanded that Alexei replace Nicholas as the tsar.

7. Soviet economic planning in the 1930s

    A. was overly rigid but overall set realistic production goals and growth rates.

    B. used the earliest analog computers to balance economic inputs and outputs.

    C. set unrealistically large production goals and often treated failure as treason.

    D. set intentionally modest production targets that could be easily exceeded.

8. All of the following contributed to the beginning of the Cold War EXCEPT:

   A. Longstanding mistrust between Soviet Communists and Western leaders
   B. The Soviet Union's determination to continue its occupation of Eastern Europe
   C. Stalin's refusal to de-Nazify its occupation zone in Germany and to try war criminals
   D. Stalin's attempt to Sovietize Greece in 1946-1949 and annex parts of Iran in 1946

9. What happened during the "July Days" of 1917?

   A. Monarchists temporarily arrested Lenin and Trotsky.
   B. Anarchists tried to assassinate the leading Bolsheviks.
   C. The Bolsheviks unsuccessfully attempted to seize power.
   D. The Kadets purged the Petrograd Soviet of pro-Bolshevik deputies.

10. What was the effect of the New Economic Policy on Russia's peasant farmers?

    A. They were not affected because NEP applied only to large-scale urban industry.
    B. They were impoverished by Stalin's policy of excessive taxation of grain surplus.
    C. They prospered because of lower grain taxes and the resumption of private trade.
    D. They prospered culturally but were impoverished by NEP's collectivization drive.

11. The key objective of Stalin's GULAG camps was to

    A. neutralize and punish political enemies while the state benefited from their labor.
    B. make a profit from the prisoners' labor, while treating them relatively humanely.
    C. house inmates temporarily until they could be murdered and buried in secret.
    D. force prisoners to learn Marxism and be reintegrated into the socialist system.

12. The Bolshevik Party evolved from the

    A. Russian Social Democratic Workers' Party.
    B. Socialist Revolutionary Party.
    C. Union of the Russian People.
    D. Constitutional Democratic Party.

13. What happened to Russia's heavy industry during NEP?

    A. It was temporarily returned to its pre-1917 owners.
    B. It was retained under state ownership and control.
    C. It was leased out to investors from Germany and the U.S.
    D. It was confiscated from owners who were disloyal.

14. Which of the following was NOT an important motivation for the Soviet collectivization drive in the late 1920s?

    A. Building socialism while at the same time destroying private property entrenched in villages
    B. Forcing peasant farmers to sell grain at low prices so that the Soviet government could feed urban workers
    C. Creating a stable food supply to maintain and expand a large army necessary to deter enemy invasions
    D. Reducing the number of Russian peasant villages because of the peasants' strongly nationalist sentiments

15. A Soviet nuclear weapon was first created in

    A. 1945.
    B. 1953.
    C. 1960.
    D. 1949.

16. Which of the following best describes late imperial Russia's religious policies?

    A. They supported Russian Orthodoxy as the official state religion.
    B. They extended full tolerance to Judaism and other non-Christian faiths.
    C. They secularized public schools and universities but not private ones.
    D. They mended the ancient schism with the Roman Catholic Church.

17. What was the result of Stalin's industrialization drive?

A. It jump-started Soviet heavy industry but involved high costs and sacrifices.

B. Russian nationalist reaction caused Stalin to abandon the worst excesses.

C. It was originally a failure but improved once free labor was introduced.

D. It was a complete failure and the Soviet economy largely deindustrialized by 1941.

18. Russia's peasant agriculture under the Old Regime was

A. growing rapidly and known as the "Peasant Miracle."

B. growing modestly and providing grain surplus for export.

C. stagnant aside from the fertile lands in northeast Russia.

D. depressed and requiring food imports from the United States.

19. The term "Cosmopolitans" in post-war Soviet propaganda referred to

A. intellectuals, many of them Jewish, deemed to be too friendly toward the West.

B. communists who thought that the Soviet victory would bring a worldwide revolution.

C. communist intellectuals who were displaced or lost their homes during the war.

D. anti-communist activists who wanted to bring the USSR into the United Nations.

20. The Belavezha Accords of 1991 declared that

A. Russia would be permitted to station troops in Poland.

B. Russia would pursue an affiliated status within NATO.

C. the Commonwealth of Independent States (CIS) would replace the USSR.

D. Russia, Belarus, and Ukraine would form the National Slavic Union.

21. Targets of Stalin's Terror in the 1930s included all of these groups EXCEPT:

   A. Individuals trained or educated in their professions before 1917
   B. Communists who at one point opposed Stalin's policies or power
   C. Individuals previously arrested as kulaks or who had served the Whites
   D. Jewish intellectuals and doctors regarded as potential enemy spies

22. Khrushchev gained and preserved his power by appealing primarily to

   A. the Central Committee of the Party, as well as the army and the KGB.
   B. technical experts who ran the Soviet Union's vast military-industrial complex.
   C. communists from Ukraine, Georgia, and the Baltic republics.
   D. grass-roots local Communist organizations who wanted reform.

23. All of the following contributed to the fall of the Soviet Union EXCEPT:

   A. Terrorist attacks
   B. Low oil prices
   C. Chernobyl accident
   D. The Spitak earthquake in 1988

24. As a result of the Winter War of 1939–1940, Finland was

   A. defeated and incorporated into the Soviet Union together with the Baltic states.
   B. victorious, inducing Stalin to accept pre-war borders and economic concessions.
   C. defeated after prolonged and brave resistance and deprived of the region of Karelia.
   D. victorious after the British and French armies landed in Narvik and rescued the Finns.

25. The 1975 Helsinki agreements required the Soviet government to

A. release all remaining POWs.
B. stop supporting terrorism.
C. observe human rights.
D. allow private small businesses.

26. Khrushchev's attitude toward the United States is best described as believing

A. that the USSR had to use its tactical nukes to demonstrate resolve.
B. in "peaceful coexistence" while pursuing a nuclear and space program.
C. in "rollback", i.e., forcefully expanding the Soviet sphere of influence.
D. that the USSR had to adopt some elements of American democracy.

27. In contemporary Russia, Gorbachev is regarded mostly as a

A. mad fanatic because he stuck to his Communist beliefs to the end.
B. great success because he ended the Cold War without violence.
C. Russia's greatest ruler because he overthrew the Communist Party.
D. failure because perestroika failed to preserve the Soviet Union.

28. Brezhnev-era investments in infrastructure

A. included nationwide transportation and energy networks and industrial modernization.
B. were limited to high-tech industries, especially electronics.
C. focused on consumer goods, to the detriment of military industry.
D. focused on oil and gas extraction, to the detriment of all other areas.

29. The main strategy of the Provisional Government was to

   A. postpone major reforms until the Constitutional Assembly was elected and the war won.

   B. call for British, French, and American military help to suppress Bolshevik uprisings.

   C. improve land and labor laws so as to win the majority in the Constitutional Assembly

   D. conclude a separate peace treaty with Germany and then carry out land reforms.

30. The "Velvet Revolution" of 1989 took place in

   A. Czechoslovakia

   B. East Germany

   C. Hungary

   D. Bulgaria

31. What was the condition of the Red Army on the eve of the German invasion in 1941?

   A. It lacked enough soldiers because the invasion was so sudden.

   B. It was completely demoralized after the defeat at Nomonhan against Japan.

   C. It was well-motivated but armed entirely with obsolete armor and aircraft.

   D. It was well-armed but weakened by purges and organizational problems.

32. Gorbachev's perestroika in 1987–1990 meant

   A. retaining the planned economy but radically reducing military expenses.

   B. easing censorship, ending the planned economy, and improving relations with the West.

   C. disbanding the Communist Party and dismantling the Warsaw Pact.

   D. permitting non-Communist parties but tougher policies toward the U.S.

33. The Soviet breakup with China happened because Mao Zedong thought

    A. the Soviet Union was irresponsible in almost starting a world war over Cuba.
    B. de-Stalinization was wrong and Khrushchev had failed to stand up to the U.S.
    C. Khrushchev was too aggressive in attempting to restart the Korean War.
    D. Khrushchev's Secret Speech failed to apologize for Stalin's purges of ethnic Chinese.

34. Reagan's reaction to the Soviet shoot-down of Korean Air Lines Flight 007 in 1983 was to

    A. admit that the flight was intended to probe Soviet air defenses.
    B. recognize that the shoot-down was negligent but not intentional.
    C. sharply criticize it as an intentional "crime against humanity."
    D. threaten the USSR with military action if it did not offer compensation.

35. Soviet policies in the 1920s with respect to national minorities

    A. continued tsarist policies of oppression and ignored minorities' needs.
    B. made an exception for national minorities when introducing socialist policies.
    C. assumed that non-Russian identities would naturally die out under socialism.
    D. promoted minority cultures and identities as long as they adhered to socialism.

36. The USSR participated in the Arab-Israeli Wars of 1967 and 1973 by

    A. providing financial and diplomatic assistance to Israel.
    B. providing massive military and other aid to the Arabs.
    C. officially refusing to be involved but secretly helping both sides.
    D. sending large numbers of ground troops disguised as Cubans.

37. Which of the following was NOT a site of a major ethnic or national conflict in the early 1990s?

A. Nagorno-Karabakh

B. Transnistria

C. South Ossetia

D. The Don Cossack District

38. What was the extent of "proxy wars" under Khrushchev?

A. The USSR and the U.S. fought proxy wars in Namibia, Iran, and Guatemala.

B. The Soviet Union trained and armed the Democratic Army of Greece in 1946.

C. Conflict in the Suez Canal prompted Khrushchev to threaten to launch nuclear missiles against the British and French.

D. USSR-trained forces in Eastern Europe fought against pro-U.S. guerillas.

39. After promising to invade Japan in August 1945, Stalin

A. broke his promise because the USSR had a nonaggression pact with Japan.

B. declared war on Japan but never commenced active operations.

C. kept his promise and defeated Japan's powerful Kwantung army.

D. attacked Japan as promised but also fought against Nationalist China.

40. All of the following are true of the Hungarian Uprising EXCEPT:

A. It began as a student-lead revolt

B. It ended in a violent Soviet silencing of opposition

C. It left 200,000 Hungarians as refugees

D. It dismantled the Warsaw Pact

41. What changed in the status of the Russian Orthodox Church in 1941–1945?

    A. It was blamed for the German invasion and almost all churches were closed.
    B. It was allowed to function as long as it promoted prayers for Communism and Stalin.
    C. It was greatly expanded and revived to provide support for the war effort.
    D. It was reestablished as the Soviet Union's official religion under Stalin's tutelage.

42. Which Eastern European nation was most pro-Soviet after 1945?

    A. Hungary
    B. Czechoslovakia
    C. Poland
    D. Romania

43. What caused the famine of 1932–1933 in the Soviet Union?

    A. A bad harvest in 1932 that could not be helped by any amount of state aid
    B. Stalin's desire to break the peasants' resistance to collectivization
    C. Stalin's desire to ethnically cleanse the Soviet Union of Ukrainians and Kazakhs
    D. Stalin's paranoia that peasants were sheltering anarchist leaders

44. When the U.S. invited Stalin to participate in the Marshall Plan, he

    A. accepted the offer unconditionally because the USSR needed all the aid it could get.
    B. refused the offer except for the U.S. program of food assistance in Ukraine.
    C. accepted the offer, as long as the USSR's planned economy would not be threatened.
    D. refused the offer when he learned about the Plan's terms.

45. The White Movement during the Russian Civil War was a

A. mass movement of peasants who resented both the Bolsheviks and their former noble masters.

B. coalition of regional governments who wanted to divide Russia into separate republics.

C. small, disciplined group of monarchist conspirators who supported Grand Duke Michael.

D. coalition of anti-Bolshevik forces that included monarchists, liberals, and the socialist revolutionists.

46. The large-scale Soviet military presence in Afghanistan ended in

A. 1988, after the Geneva Agreements with the U.S.

B. 1985, as soon as Gorbachev came to power.

C. 1991, as soon as the Soviet Union fell.

D. 1984, after U.S. Stinger missiles grounded Soviet aircraft.

47. The Treaty of Rapallo of 1922 involved mutual diplomatic recognition between the USSR and

A. Fascist Italy.

B. Weimar Germany.

C. Kemalist Turkey.

D. Republican Spain.

48. The Berlin Blockade of 1948–1949 was

A. a miscalculation by Stalin because the Western bloc did not back down.

B. inconclusive because the Soviet Army continued to control West Berlin.

C. a victory for Stalin because his authority in East Germany was strengthened.

D. a major defeat for Stalin because he had to allow U.S. observers into East Berlin.

49. Mikhail Gorbachev came to power because he

A. was viewed by the aging Politburo as a younger, more energetic type of leader.

B. promised to do everything in his power to overthrow Communism in Russia.

C. promised to do everything in his power to preserve Communism in Russia.

D. was viewed by the Politburo as an ignorant upstart who could be easily dominated.

50. How extensive was the Holocaust in the Soviet Union?

A. The Germans were more lenient towards Soviet Jews, as opposed to Polish Jews.

B. Most Soviet Jews were forewarned and managed to escape to the East.

C. Most of the Jews in German-occupied territory were killed, totaling between 2 and 3 million.

D. The Germans spared those Jews who openly condemned Stalin and Communism.

51. The extent of Soviet participation in the Korean War was that it

A. sent over 250,000 Soviet Army "volunteers" masquerading as Chinese troops.

B. refused to support North Korea and antagonized Mao Zedong's China.

C. financed and armed North Korea, sent military advisers, and provided air cover.

D. supported North Korea only diplomatically and by promising economic aid.

52. Who was the most likely successor to Stalin in 1953?

A. Marshal Zhukov

B. Leonid Brezhnev

C. Lavrentiy Beria

D. Vyacheslav Molotov

53. Socialist Realist art under Stalin meant

A. returning to traditional realist forms while glorifying new communist values.

B. discarding communist ideology and relying on traditional pre-1917 artistic forms.

C. avoiding any realistic subjects and developing unique, ideology-driven artistic forms.

D. continuing the Avant-Garde art of the 1920s but depicting working-class subjects.

54. Which of the following most accurately describes the cultural "Thaw" under Khrushchev?

A. It was a propagandistic fiction, because Thaw leaders were coached to appear independent.

B. It proceeded in fits and starts, with liberal waves replaced by conservative attacks.

C. Political topics could be discussed but only in Aesopian language.

D. The topic of Stalin's terror was freely discussed in print under Khrushchev.

55. Gorbachev's 1988 Law on Cooperatives

A. for the first time permitted private businesses to use hired labor.

B. prohibited most forms of private business as contrary to glasnost.

C. allowed private business under oversight from state-owned organizations.

D. allowed private business as long as hired labor was not "exploited."

56. Most of the intellectuals known as "dissidents"

A. emphasized right-wing versions of ethnic Russian nationalism.

B. wanted the Soviet government to accurately observe its own laws.

C. used terror to overthrow the government for their personal gain.

D. thought that socialism as an ideology was completely wrong-headed.

57. The only anti-Communist revolution in Eastern Europe in 1989 that involved largescale violence took place in

A. Poland.
B. Hungary.
C. Bulgaria.
D. Romania.

58. U.S. support of Islamist fighters in Afghanistan began

A. never, because the U.S. only supported the secular opposition.
B. a few months before the Soviet invasion in 1979.
C. a few months after the Soviet invasion in 1979.
D. only in 1982 after the Soviets appeared to be winning.

59. The Soviet war in Afghanistan can be best described as a

A. clear win because Islamic militancy was contained.
B. clear loss because it led directly to the Soviet collapse.
C. military success but political failure because the Afghan population was antagonized.
D. military failure but political success because the Afghan population was won over.

60. Brezhnev-era "stagnation" refers to the fact that

A. the Soviet middle class became increasingly impoverished.
B. Soviet military equipment was inferior to that of the U.S.
C. Soviet culture and the arts lacked vitality and originality.
D. the rate of Soviet economic growth was slowing down.

ANSWER KEY AND EXPLANATIONS

1. A	13. B	25. C	37. D	49. A
2. C	14. D	26. B	38. C	50. C
3. A	15. D	27. D	39. C	51. C
4. B	16. A	28. A	40. D	52. C
5. A	17. A	29. A	41. C	53. A
6. C	18. B	30. A	42. B	54. B
7. C	19. A	31. D	43. B	55. A
8. C	20. C	32. B	44. D	56. B
9. C	21. D	33. B	45. D	57. D
10. C	22. A	34. C	46. A	58. B
11. A	23. A	35. D	47. B	59. C
12. A	24. C	36. B	48. A	60. D

1. **The correct answer is A.** The USSR was given about one-third of Eastern Prussia as part of its share of war reparations from Germany. While Western Allies were uneasy about the USSR's continued occupation of some of its gains from 1939–1940 (such as the Baltic Republics), these gains were de facto recognized by the Yalta Agreement.

2. **The correct answer is C.** Freedom of speech was not introduced during the Great Reforms. Choices A, B, and D are incorrect because all of these items were part of the Great Reforms.

3. **The correct answer is A.** The Germans failed to capture Leningrad but cut it off from most supplies, so that over 600,000 of its citizens died of starvation. Choice B is incorrect because Leningrad was never captured. Choice C is incorrect because Leningrad was not a temporary capital during that period. Choice D is incorrect because Tankograd was located in Chelyabinsk in the Urals, and not in Leningrad.

4. **The correct answer is B.** Russia's heavy industry and railroad network grew particularly rapidly in the 1890s. For this reason, choice A is incorrect. Choice C is incorrect because industry did not stagnate. Choice D is incorrect because industry did not decline and Old Believer merchants supported capitalism rather than opposed it.

5. **The correct answer is A.** The Russian army suffered its most serious defeats during the munitions shortages in 1915. Choice B is incorrect because Russia did not suffer manpower shortages during the First World War. Choice C is incorrect because lack of naval power did not seriously hinder Russia's war effort. Choice D is incorrect because fortresses did not play a significant role in Russia's war effort.

6. **The correct answer is C.** The tsar's government lost control of Petrograd after food shortages led to strikes and violent riots and the city's garrison had rebelled as well. Choice A is incorrect because Germans were not threatening Petrograd in February 1917. Choice B is incorrect because Rasputin's assassination occurred months before the revolution and did not lead to anti-clerical riots. Choice D is incorrect because the Petrograd garrison did not want Nicholas' son, Alexei, to be the next tsar.

7. **The correct answer is C.** Soviet five-year plans were impossible to meet because of their unrealistic goals. Choice A is incorrect because production goals were not realistic. Choice B is incorrect because computer-assisted calculations were not used. Choice D is incorrect because production targets were excessively high rather than modest.

8. **The correct answer is C.** Stalin did not refuse to de-Nazify its occupation zone or to try war criminals. Choices A, B, and D were all factors in worsening relations between the USSR and the Western Allies.

9. **The correct answer is C.** In July 1917, the Bolsheviks tried to seize power in the wake of popular uprisings, but failed. Choice A is incorrect because monarchists were not a major political force in Petrograd. Choice B is incorrect because no one tried to assassinate Bolshevik leaders. Choice D is incorrect because it was the Kadets who were purged after the July days.

10. **The correct answer is C.** NEP involved a much better treatment of peasants by the Bolshevik government. Choice A is incorrect because NEP policies did not apply to largescale industry. Choice B is incorrect because peasants were not impoverished under NEP and excessive taxation was not one of NEP's features. Choice D is incorrect because NEP did not involve a collectivization drive.

11. **The correct answer is A.** Stalin's GULAG camps were punitive in nature, but at the same time were intended to contribute economically by providing labor for those sectors to which free labor could not be easily attracted. Choice B is incorrect because GULAG prisoners were not treated humanely. Choice C is incorrect because GULAG camps were not set up to intentionally murder large numbers of inmates. Choice D is incorrect because reeducation was occasionally an element of GULAG camps but a very minor one.

12. **The correct answer is A.** The Russian Social Democratic Workers' Party split off into Bolshevik and Menshevik branches. Choices B, C, and D are incorrect because these were different political parties not related to the Bolsheviks.

13. **The correct answer is B.** NEP's policy of economic liberalization did not apply to heavy industry. Choice A is incorrect because heavy industry was not privatized. Choice C is incorrect because heavy industry was not leased out to foreign firms. Choice D is incorrect because all heavy industry in Russia had been nationalized in 1918–1919.

14. **The correct answer is D.** Peasants' nationalism was not a major concern during collectivization. Choices A, B, and C are incorrect because these items were all among the reasons for undertaking the collectivization of Soviet agriculture.

15. **The correct answer is D.** The Soviet nuclear bomb was tested in 1949. For this reason, choices A, B, and C are incorrect.

16. **The correct answer is A.** Russian Orthodoxy was the official state-supported religion in the Russian Empire. Other religions were tolerated to a limited extent. Choice B is incorrect because non-Christian faiths and Judaism in particular did not enjoy full tolerance. Choice C is incorrect because public schools required mandatory catechism lessons. Choice D is incorrect because the official policy was not striving to mend the schism between the Orthodox and Catholic churches.

17. **The correct answer is A.** Stalin's industrialization made Soviet industry the second-largest after that of the U.S. but at a high cost in human lives and suffering. Choice B is incorrect because there was no Russian nationalist reaction. Choice C is incorrect because, while free labor was used alongside GULAG inmates on most major sites, it did not ensure that industrialization was a success. Choice D is not correct because only a few of the Soviet industrial projects of the 1930s can be described as clear failures.

18. **The correct answer is B.** While per capita incomes in late imperial Russia were low, its vast agricultural sector was growing modestly, and Russia was the world's leading wheat exporter. Choice A is incorrect because Russian agriculture did not grow rapidly. Choice C is incorrect because agriculture was not stagnant and northeast Russia was not fertile. Choice D is incorrect because domestic food supplies were sufficient under the Old Regime.

19. **The correct answer is A.** The campaign against "rootless cosmopolitanism" was intended to root out any support or sympathy for the West among Soviet elites. Choices B, C, and D are incorrect because these groups were not specified as targets of the campaign against cosmopolitans.

20. **The correct answer is C.** The 1991 agreement among the leaders of the Russian Federation, Ukraine, and Belarus in effect disbanded the Soviet Union and replaced it with the CIS. Choices A, B, and D were not issues addressed by the Belavezha Accords.

21. The correct answer is D. Jewish intellectuals and doctors were targeted in the late 1940s and early 1950s but not during the pre-war terror. Choices A, B, and C are incorrect because all of these groups were targeted in the 1930s.

22. The correct answer is A. Khrushchev maintained his power by reaffirming the privileged position of the Communist Party and its Central Committee. In addition, he was supported by important military and KGB figures who did not want a return of Stalinist politics. Choice B is incorrect because technical experts were sidelined under Khrushchev. Choice C is incorrect because non-Russian leaders were not regarded as a significant source of support in their own right. Choice D is incorrect because there were no independent grassroots Communist organizations under Khrushchev.

23. The correct answer is A. Terrorist attacks did occur in the Soviet Union in the 1970s and 1980s but they were not frequent enough or violent enough to undermine the Soviet regime. Choice B is incorrect because low oil prices deprived the USSR of its source of hard currency. Choice C is incorrect because the Chernobyl nuclear accident was expensive and undermined public confidence in the Communist Party. Choice D is incorrect because the Spitak earthquake in Armenia was hugely expensive to repair and thus damaged the Soviet economy.

24. The correct answer is C. Although Finland put up a good fight, it was defeated and lost some of its territory in Karelia. Choice A is incorrect because the USSR failed to annex Finland. Choice B is incorrect because Finland did not win the war. Choice D is incorrect because the British and the French did not join the war on the Finns' side, although they did send some weapons and supplies.

25. The correct answer is C. The Soviet Union agreed to observe human rights. Choice A is incorrect because POWs were not an issue in 1975. Choice B is incorrect because in Helsinki, the USSR was not accused of supporting terrorism. Choice D is incorrect because private business was not a topic discussed at Helsinki.

26. **The correct answer is B.** Khrushchev believed that nuclear war was not inevitable, but he was determined to build up Soviet nuclear and missile strength. Choice A is incorrect because Khrushchev did not want to use nuclear weapons. Choice C is incorrect because he did not believe in a forceful "rollback" of the Western bloc, although he did suppress attempts to reduce Soviet influence in Eastern Europe. Choice D is incorrect because there was no question of adopting American democracy even in part.

27. **The correct answer is D.** In today's Russia, Gorbachev is widely criticized for failing to preserve the Soviet Union. Choice A is incorrect because it is not commonly believed that Gorbachev did stick to his Communist beliefs. Choice B is incorrect because Gorbachev's role in ending the Cold War is not widely viewed as an accomplishment in Russia, because he failed to secure terms advantageous to the Soviet Union. Choice C is incorrect because Gorbachev is not viewed as a great (or the greatest) ruler or as having intentionally overthrown the Communist Party.

28. **The correct answer is A.** Brezhnev-era investments emphasized long-term capital projects. Choice B is incorrect because investments went to all areas, and electronics were not privileged. Choice C is incorrect because military industry still had priority. Choice D is incorrect because oil and gas were important, but other areas of the economy were being developed as well.

29. **The correct answer is A.** The Provisional Government was formed to run the country until nationwide elections could be held and to make sure that the war effort was maintained. Choice B is incorrect because Bolshevik uprisings were not originally seen as a major threat and foreign assistance was not requested. Choice C is incorrect because the Provisional Government refused to introduce major social reforms. Choice D is incorrect because the Provisional Government ruled out both a separate peace and land reform.

30. **The correct answer is A.** The term "Velvet Revolution" is applied to Czechoslovakia's overthrow of Communism in 1989. Choices B, C, and D are incorrect.

31. **The correct answer is D.** The Red Army had sufficient numbers of modern weapons, but its morale and organization were weakened by the purges and rapid expansion in the late 1930s. Choice A is incorrect because the Red Army was not smaller than the German Army. Choice B is incorrect because the Red Army won the battle of Nomonhan. Choice C is incorrect because the Red Army had large numbers of modern weapons in addition to even larger numbers of out-of-date ones.

32. **The correct answer is B.** Important aspects of Gorbachev's policies were glasnost (the relaxation of censorship), permitting private business, and easing the USSR's confrontation with the West. Choice A is incorrect because the planned economy was widely seen as untenable. Choice C is incorrect because perestroika was meant to preserve the Communist system. Choice D is incorrect because perestroika involved a more conciliatory policy toward the U.S.

33. **The correct answer is B.** Mao broke with Khrushchev over his de-Stalinization and because he failed to respond more forcefully to the crisis with the U-2 spy plane in 1960. Choice A is incorrect because the Cuban crisis happened after the break with China. Choice C is incorrect because Khrushchev did not attempt to restart the Korean War. Choice D is incorrect because purges of ethnic Chinese people or a failure to apologize for them were not a factor in the Sino-Soviet rift.

34. **The correct answer is C.** Reagan criticized the incident as if it were an intentional murder of civilians by the Soviets. Choice A is incorrect because Reagan never admitted that the CIA may have been involved in the incident. Choice B is incorrect because Reagan claimed that the Soviets knew that the plane was full of civilians. Choice D is incorrect because Reagan did not threaten to go to war with the USSR over this incident.

35. **The correct answer is D.** Bolshevik nationalities policy in the 1920s reversed the tsars' policy of Russification and promoted national and ethnic minority cultures. Choice A is incorrect because tsarist nationalist policies did not always involve oppression and in any case were not imitated in the 1920s. Choice B is incorrect because no significant exceptions were made for national minorities. Choice C is incorrect because Stalin believed that national identities would survive even after the USSR became fully socialist.

36. **The correct answer is B.** The Soviet Union provided massive military aid to Egypt, Syria, and other Arab countries. Choice A is incorrect because the USSR only supported Israel briefly and indirectly in the late 1940s. Choice C is incorrect because the Soviet Union openly supported the Arabs. Choice D is incorrect because the Soviet Union sent pilots, sailors, and surface-to-air missiles to assist the Arabs but no ground troops, disguised or otherwise.

37. **The correct answer is D.** Don Cossacks are not usually regarded to be an ethnic or a national group, and they were not directly involved in any conflicts. Choices A, B, and C are incorrect because all of these areas involved inter-ethnic conflicts in the early 1990s.

38. **The correct answer is C.** The Cold War under Khrushchev focused on the space and nuclear race and on maintaining Soviet control in Eastern Europe; however, he did back the Egyptian leader when he nationalized the Suez Canal. After the British and French supported Israel in its attack on Egypt, Khrushchev threatened to launch a nuclear attack on all three nations. Choices A, B, and D are incorrect because these conflicts did not take place under Khrushchev's regime.

39. **The correct answer is C.** The USSR invaded Japan and defeated its forces in Manchuria and North China. Choice A is incorrect because the USSR abrogated its nonaggression pact with Japan when it attacked in August 1945. Choice B is incorrect because the Red Army did actively attack the Japanese forces. Choice D is incorrect because the Red Army did not fight against Nationalist Chinese forces in 1945.

40. **The correct answer is D.** The uprising was unsuccessful and the Warsaw Pact remained intact. Choice A is incorrect because the Hungarian Uprising began as a student revolt as an attempt to deflect from the Warsaw Pact. Choice B is incorrect as it ended in Soviet troops crushing the opposition. Choice C is incorrect because the uprising did indeed result in 200,000 Hungarian refugees.

41. **The correct answer is C.** Stalin's policy was to expand and support the Church during the war. Choice A is incorrect because the Church was not blamed for the German invasion. Choice B is incorrect because praying for Stalin and Communism were not conditions for allowing the Church to revive its organization. Choice D is incorrect because the Russian Orthodox Church was greatly strengthened during the war, but it was not made an official church.

42. **The correct answer is B.** Czechoslovakia's leaders and ruling elites were relatively well disposed toward the USSR after 1945. Other Eastern European countries were much less friendly, so choices A, C, and D are incorrect.

43. **The correct answer is B.** The key cause of the famine was the government's policy of forced collectivization and its determination to overcome the peasants' resistance by confiscating a large proportion (up to 40 percent) of their 1932 harvest. Choice A is incorrect because the harvest in 1932 was bad but not catastrophically so. Choice C is incorrect because Stalin's hostility was toward peasants as socially alien elements and not toward any particular ethnic groups. Choice D is incorrect because anarchist leaders were not a major concern at that time.

44. **The correct answer is D.** Stalin considered accepting the Marshall Plan in the form of a money loan from the U.S. but declined when he found out the details of its terms. Choices A and C are incorrect because Stalin did not accept the Plan. Choice B is incorrect because there was no U.S. program to assist Ukraine.

45. **The correct answer is D.** The White Movement consisted of numerous organizations and armies of different political persuasions. Choice A is incorrect because the Whites failed to secure the loyalty of large numbers of peasants. Choice B is incorrect because major White leaders wanted to preserve a single and indivisible Russia. Choice C is incorrect because monarchists were not the only members of the White Movement. Grand Duke Michael had been killed in 1918 and so could not take part in it.

46. **The correct answer is A.** The U.S. and the USSR agreed to end their respective involvement in Afghanistan in 1988. Choice B is incorrect because Gorbachev initially wanted to escalate the war, not end it. Choice C is incorrect because Soviet involvement ended long before the fall of the Soviet Union. Choice D is incorrect because the Soviets suffered from the Stinger missiles supplied to the mujahedeen but quickly captured a sample missile and developed countermeasures.

47. **The correct answer is B.** The Treaty of Rapallo was a landmark agreement between Soviet Russia and Weimar Germany. Choices A, C, and D are incorrect because these countries were not parties to the Treaty of Rapallo.

48. **The correct answer is A.** Stalin expected that the U.S. and its allies would meet his demand and did not anticipate that they would instead run an airlift. Choice B is incorrect because the Soviet Army did not control West Berlin. Choice C is incorrect because his authority in East Germany was weakened, rather than strengthened, as a result of the blockade. Choice D is incorrect because Stalin neither suffered a major defeat nor had to allow U.S. observers into East Berlin.

49. The correct answer is A. Gorbachev was promoted because he was seen as younger and more energetic but holding the same beliefs and values as his older comrades. Choices B and C are incorrect because overthrowing or maintaining Communism was not an issue in deciding whether Gorbachev would become the next leader. Choice D is incorrect because Gorbachev was recognized as intelligent and well-connected to influential older Communists.

50. The correct answer is C. While many Jews did escape the German onslaught, most of those who stayed behind were killed. Choice A is incorrect because the Germans were equally brutal toward Soviet and Polish Jews. Choice B is incorrect because most Soviet Jews were unable to escape the Germans in time to save themselves. Choice D is incorrect because the Germans were not interested in recruiting collaborators from among Soviet Jews.

51. The correct answer is C. The USSR sponsored North Korea and provided fighter aircraft and pilots. Choice A is incorrect because Soviet troops did not intervene in large numbers. Choice B is incorrect because Stalin actually did support North Korea. Choice D is incorrect because Stalin also provided considerable military aid.

52. The correct answer is C. Until his arrest and likely murder on June 26, 1953, Lavrentiy Beria was the most powerful figure in the Soviet Union. Choice A is incorrect because Zhukov was removed from active political life during Stalin's last years. Choice B is incorrect because Brezhnev was too junior to succeed Stalin. Choice D is incorrect because Molotov had been disgraced by Stalin and removed as a likely successor.

53. The correct answer is A. Writers and other cultural figures were expected to glorify communism while using traditional forms that would be easily appreciated by workers and peasants. Choice B is incorrect because communist ideology was not to be discarded. Choice C is incorrect because realistic forms and subjects were required. Choice D is incorrect because the Avant-Garde art of the 1920s was viewed with suspicion in the 1930s and largely avoided.

54. **The correct answer is B.** There were several periods of cultural liberalization, known as the Thaw, always followed by periods of tighter censorship and attacks in the press by conservative intellectuals. Choice A is incorrect because the Thaw was a real event. Choice C is incorrect because many important political problems were discussed directly (if only intermittently). Choice D is incorrect because Stalin's terror was discussed in print but in carefully measured ways.

55. **The correct answer is A.** Private businesses, labeled as cooperatives, were allowed to function virtually without restrictions. Choices B, C, and D are incorrect because none of these restrictions applied under the terms of the 1988 law.

56. **The correct answer is B.** Dissidents demanded above all that the Soviet government at least observe the laws that it itself issued. Choice A is incorrect because right-wing Russian nationalist dissidents were few in number. Choice C is incorrect because dissidents did not use terror. Choice D is incorrect because dissidents did not oppose socialism.

57. **The correct answer is D.** Mass violence took place in Romania only. For this reason, choices A, B, and C are incorrect.

58. **The correct answer is B.** The U.S. began to support Islamist forces in Afghanistan approximately six months before the Soviet invasion. Choice A is incorrect because there was no significant secular opposition in Afghanistan during the period in question, and the U.S. supported the Islamic opposition (mujahedeen). Choice C is incorrect because the U.S. started to support the mujahedeen hoping to undermine Soviet influence before the actual invasion. Choice D is incorrect because the U.S. started to support the mujahedeen long before 1982.

59. **The correct answer is C.** The Soviet Army won all major battles and operations but was unable to secure Afghanistan's pro-Soviet regime politically. Choice A is incorrect because Islamic militancy continued to grow in the 1980s. Choice B is incorrect because the war was only a minor factor in undermining Gorbachev's power. Choice D is incorrect because the Soviets failed to win over Afghanistan's population.

60. **The correct answer is D.** The Soviet economy was growing under Brezhnev but not fast enough to ensure parity with the West. Choice A is incorrect because the Soviet middle class was much better off under Brezhnev than ever before. Choice B is incorrect because Soviet weapons were often equal or superior to American ones. Choice C is incorrect because the Soviet Union developed brilliant artistic and cultural productions under Brezhnev.

Printed in the USA
CPSIA information can be obtained
at www.ICGtesting.com
JSHW012042140824
68134JS00033B/3214